# Inside Network Marketing

## An Expert's View into the Hidden Truths and Exploited Myths of America's Most Misunderstood Industry

**Revised and Updated 2nd Edition**

LEONARD W. CLEMENTS

**Prima Publishing**

3000 Lava Ridge Court • Roseville, California 95661
(800) 632-8676 • www.primalifestyles.com

PRIMA PUBLISHING and colophon are trademarks of Prima Communications Inc., registered with the United States Patent and Trademark Office.

**Library of Congress Cataloging-in-Publication Data**
Clements, Leonard W.
Inside network marketing : an expert's view into the hidden truths and exploited myths of America's most misunderstood industry / Leonard W. Clements.—Rev. and updated 2nd ed.
    p.    cm.
Includes bibliographical references and index.
ISBN 0-7615-2176-3
1. Multilevel marketing.    I. Title.
HF5415.126.C54    2000
658.8'4—dc21                                                    99-057314
                                                                      CIP

00 01 02 03 HH 10 9 8 7 6 5 4 3 2 1

Printed in the United States of America

**How to Order**
Single copies may be ordered from Prima Publishing, 3000 Lava Ridge Court, Roseville, CA 95661; telephone (800) 632-8676. Quantity discounts are also available. On your letterhead, include information concerning the intended use of the books and the number of books you wish to purchase.

**Visit us online at www.primalifestyles.com**

# CONTENTS

**CHAPTER THREE**

**What We Should Not Be Doing (But Are)  149**

**CHAPTER FOUR**

**The Numbers Game  213**

THIS IS A BOOK that tells the truth about network marketing. Now, ask yourself, "Is that really what I want to hear?"

I can understand if you don't. "As scarce as the truth is," Josh Billings once observed, "the supply has always been in excess of demand."

Well, if it's other than the truth about network marketing you're after, look elsewhere, for Len Clements is one who agonizes over getting his facts straight and right and accurately stated.

Len is the classic student. He researches everything. Talks to everybody. Thinks before he opinionates. Four good reasons to pay close attention to what he writes. I pay very close attention to Len. His *MarketWave* newsletter is the only publication I read from cover to cover. In truth—and I suppose it's because I spend so much time writing it—I read Len's work more than my own. But then, I'm a student too. And I've found him to be a deeper teacher than most on the vast and varied subject of network marketing.

In this book, you'll find lots of "straight talk" about our industry.

You'll learn a lot about why we do what we do and ways to do it better.

You'll discover new ideas that will help you build a growing and enduring organization.

You'll reveal reasons and understandings that will firm up your foundation as a leader.

You'll have access to lots of good things to say in presentations and trainings sessions.

You'll have a good time doing this, because the guy can write. Jerry Rubin once told me Len Clements was his favorite network marketing writer. I didn't take that as a slight. He's mine, too.

There's an old proverb about truth that warns you, Tell the truth—and run! I know in the past, Len has caught a good deal of flack for taking a stand for what he thinks and deeply feels works and doesn't work in network marketing. The price of passion.

Michael Gerber taught me that passion comes from love. I can tell you this about Len and what he says and writes: It comes from an abiding love for this business and its people. That's enough for me to pay attention carefully and closely to Len's book.

Besides, as another honest writer once said, Truth takes at least two people: one to write it—one to read it.

Enjoy the book. It's a good one.

John Fogg
Editor in Chief, *Network Marketing Lifestyles*
Author of *The Greatest Networker in the World* and
*Conversations with the Greatest Networker in the World*

# ACKNOWLEDGMENTS

FIRST AND FOREMOST, my endless thanks to John Fogg and Tom Schreiter. If not for these two guys, I honestly believe that *MarketWave*, and most likely my MLM career, would not have lasted beyond the winter of 1991—and this book would most certainly not have been written.

My heartfelt gratitude goes out to all of my loyal newsletter subscribers and corporate consulting clients who, even after I "sold out" by actually joining an MLM opportunity, still trusted my objectivity and judgment.

To my many friends in this industry, I can only hope I've demonstrated that friendship well enough for you to know who you are—because I'm not about to try to list you all here (I'm too afraid I'd miss someone).

I'm also compelled to acknowledge my upline, both present and past, and all those company owners, CEOs, VPs, and presidents I've been associated with over these many years. You deserve an award for putting up with all of my "suggestions." I know I can be a pain in the butt, but I hope I've been a valuable one.

And finally, I offer my love and appreciation to my mom and dad. They are two of the most honest, ethical people I have ever known. I will always strive to be all that they are.

T HIS BOOK IS like no other book about multilevel marketing (MLM) you have ever read. It will not attempt to teach you how to get rich in this business. It will not necessarily persuade your skeptical prospect to join your MLM program. It may not motivate or inspire you to sell more products or build a bigger downline. And it certainly isn't going to tell you everything you want to hear.

What you will find in this book is the truth—the truth about the state of the MLM industry and the way this business is being practiced. You will find that the veil draped between you and network marketing hides both the good and the bad. This book attempts to expose not only wrongdoing but also those who would have you believe there is no good in network marketing (indeed, there are far more "victims" of the latter sort). This will include an abundance of information you will never find in a training video or at an opportunity meeting—and rarely even in the MLM trade publications. You are about to be educated on what kind of business you are considering or have already joined. In fact, in all modesty, I firmly believe that even the grizzled veterans of MLM who've been around this industry for 30 years or more might actually learn something new about the nature of the business, the way it's being practiced, how it has changed, and where it is going.

I intend this book to be chock-full of surprises.

Please understand right now, I am dearly in love with multilevel marketing. I am one of its biggest advocates. I would defend this industry to the teeth, in much the same way parents would defend their children. Parents would still scold and punish children if necessary—because they love them.

The network marketing industry is a child. Sure, there have been MLM companies for more than 50 years, but for all intents and purposes, the industry of multilevel marketing really began about 1980. So we're dealing with a very well-intentioned, but sometimes very troubled, and definitely very stubborn, 19-year-old; a 19-year-old with a bad reputation (more a guilt by association, really), but one that's very well loved by those who truly understand it. Unfortunately, far too many of us are abandoning it when it acts naughty, rather than scolding it and trying to teach it to be a better citizen. My hope is that the criticisms made here will be constructive ones—out of love, and with hope for a better, more productive adulthood for our industry.

It will become glaringly obvious early on in this book that its primary purpose wasn't to make the author a lot of money. Although I believe it will be perceived to be positive overall, it will nonetheless not be a book you'll likely find in any company's distributor kit, or one that will be "recommended" by a lot of upline leaders. This book will definitely lend itself to self-discovery.

Don't get the impression this is going to be a few hundred pages of MLM bashing. I'm not going to "expose" any companies here. I'm only dwelling on the negative because that's what makes this book unique; it tells both sides of the story. Actually, the positive (or just educational) material will make up the majority of these pages. I intend to have some fun with this book. I don't want it to be a downer. It can educate and even criticize and still be entertaining reading.

The format of the book is a little unusual as well. The chapters are very broad in scope, with essays on various subjects. Each essay is a reprint of my "Facts & Myths of Multilevel Marketing" column found in past issues of my newsletter. This column has also been reprinted numerous times in more than a dozen MLM trade publications both here and abroad, so some may be familiar to you. Don't skip the ones you think you may have read previously. Almost all are somewhat revised from their original version. I've either updated certain statistical information (I'm a statistics nut), or I may have just changed my mind about a certain point. Other "experts" might lead you to believe that their advice and information are all-knowing and perfect, but I admit I haven't been *completely* right about *everything* I've ever said on the subject of MLM.

Of course, I am now.

On occasion, I have also removed the names of individuals and companies. You will find, however, that in many cases I do name names. Also, each essay is preceded by an introduction explaining my motive, incentive, or impetus for writing the article. The essay is followed by a discussion describing the reaction, effect, and in some cases aftermath of the article.

There's the obligatory bio of me at the end of the book, so I won't describe my personal history right now. If, however, you feel that no one making less than $25,000 per month in this business has a right to claim any "expertise" of it, let me address this issue here and now (because unfortunately, I know there are a lot of you out there).

Personally, I consider asking professional network marketers how much money they make just as rude a question as it would be in any other form of business. I will say this: My current MLM income would probably put me in the upper 5% of all distributors in this industry. No, it's not $25,000. In fact, after finishing this book you'll probably realize that even being in the top 5% may not be that impressive. I know people in this business, however, who are obscenely rich and don't have a clue about how to do it!

Fortunately for them, one of the few people they did manage to sign up did have a clue. But then, that's the beauty of MLM, isn't it? As MLM guru Dayle Maloney says, it's not who you know, it's who *they* know. On the other hand, some of the most knowledgeable people regarding MLM make little and, in a few cases, no income from it, at least not directly from an MLM downline. One has never even been an MLM distributor!

I agree that someone who's never made $10,000 per month should not claim expertise in how to make a million dollars in MLM. But there are more forms of expertise than just how to make money. Like I said, this book isn't about getting rich. It's about getting rich with knowledge. If anything, it's more about how not to lose money in MLM. In the 20 years I've been associated with network marketing, and the 11 in which I've studied and analyzed it full time,

I've definitely gained a wealth of knowledge—and I've *never* lost any money in MLM.

As you will soon discover, I have many peeves when it comes to MLM. This ridiculous income versus expertise issue is just one of them.

Another is MLM books that don't get to the point. So let's get to the point. . . .

# CHAPTER ONE

# The State of the Industry

THE END OF 1992 and early 1993 was a bad time for me, attitude-wise. I had just written three exposés: one of downline building services, one about a German-based money-game called Euro-Round (which garnered one of four death threats I've received), and one about a company that was faking large monthly bonus checks.

I had also just written a report on a convoluted, confusing, constantly evolving program where the primary income source to the "company" was the proceeds of life insurance policies taken out by its distributors. Basically, in this business a "good month" was when a lot of its distributors died. In this program, high attrition rates were a plus! It claimed to be a multilevel marketing opportunity, and I suppose technically it was, at least in one of the several ways in which people were paid. The program involved either getting in with only a $25 fee (and earning several hundred dollars in bonuses, commissions, and life insurance and credit card payments each month), or purchasing a batch of leads for $500, of which more than 80% was paid back to the field in commissions. The entire mechanism by which this was implemented was, in my opinion, a gross corruption of the multilevel marketing (MLM) system.

Anyway, I rushed the January 1993 issue of *MarketWave* out a month early because this scheme was claiming to be signing up as many as 2,000 people per week (and I think they were), and I had no doubt this scheme would be gone before most folks took down their Christmas trees. As it turned out, I was right. A barrage of legal actions were taken in the form of federal restraining orders, state-issued cease-and-desist orders, and lawsuits by various other banking and insurance agencies (which the founder claims were all eventually dismissed—3 years later).

Right after Christmas, however, I received two phone calls in the same afternoon. One was from a subscriber to my newsletter, *MarketWave,* who claimed he had just sent in his $25 anyway, despite having read my three-page scathing review of the program. He felt the small amount was "worth the risk." The second call was from a man who I knew was not well off financially, who called to tell me he too had just read my review—and sent in the $500 anyway. He was calling to see if I *really* thought he was making a mistake! He never got his $500 back.

I remember the exact moment, after hanging up with that last caller, when I threw my pencil in the air (it actually stuck in my ceiling) and said out loud, "Why the hell am I doing this!?" After all, *MarketWave* was not yet a big money-maker either. And I sure wasn't doing it for my health. So I wasn't exactly in the greatest frame of mind.

The most definitive article I've written to date regarding the state of the MLM industry was in that same January issue. It also has by far the most negative tone, so let's get it out of the way early. Again, keep in mind it was written in 1993 and my state of mind when I wrote it.

# MLM: The Industry of the '90s?

QUICK, HIDE IN the closet! Bring a flashlight so you can read this article, but don't read aloud. Someone might hear you. And be warned, this isn't what you want to hear—or have been hearing.

For the past 3 years we have been led to believe that MLM is "the industry of the '90s!" Well, we're about a third of the way through the 1990s, and MLM is just as maligned, misunderstood, abused, criticized, and ignored as it's ever been.

The mainstream media seems to be picking up the pace of negative MLM-related stories. And why not? We're an industry that rarely advertises in the mainstream media. What do they have to lose?

Some state attorney generals (an elected position) now seem to see MLM opportunities as prime targets anytime they need to demonstrate their effectiveness. Nothing like shutting down one of those ol' pyramid schemes to get some respect and recognition from the people. Besides, the graphic in their opportunity brochure "is even shaped like a pyramid."[1] And after all, MLM distributors are just "a bunch of lemmings running around duplicating each other."[2] That's why "pyramid schemes will not be tolerated,"[3] and "pyramid marketing"[4] will be under such heavy scrutiny. They may even have to "investigate Amway"[5] since "every illegal pyramid scheme is multilevel marketing."[6]

Even the home business publications refuse to recognize MLM as a serious business opportunity. Two such publications recently published lists of the hottest home business opportunities of the 1990s. There was dog grooming. There was basket making. There was wedding planning. There was even chimney sweeping. Another listed the "top 10 businesses for the '90s." Gift baskets were listed ($11,000 start-up cost), along with financial-aid services ($12,000 start-up cost). Last year I even remember seeing a list of

---

[1] Past Michigan attorney general on national television, referring to the compensation plan diagram in a brochure of an 8-year-old, multimillion-dollar company with over 120,000 distributors—and the diagram wasn't even shaped like a pyramid! (1991)

[2] Assistant to the attorney general in Florida, referring to network marketing distributors in general. (1991)

[3] Attorney general of Virginia, referring to a service-based MLM program and other MLMs that "operate in a similar fashion." (1992)

[4] Assistant to the attorney general in Oregon, referring to network marketing in general. (1992)

[5] Investigator for the Missouri attorney general's office, before being informed that Amway was a $4 billion, 37-year-old company operating in over 60 countries (and employing several thousand people and 1.5 million distributors) that has already successfully fought years of legal battles in federal court—which he was totally unaware of! (1990)

[6] Current Michigan attorney general, apparently oblivious to the fact that "multilevel marketing" is a specific, well-established title for a legally recognized form of business. Fortunately, she didn't say all multilevel marketing operations were illegal pyramids! (1999)

"100 businesses you can start for under $500." Not one mentioned MLM. Not one!

Likewise for all the business opportunity/franchise expos I've been to. I've visited three within the last year, and although they all seem to have no problem taking the money of those network marketers who want to rent booth space, the accompanying forums, seminars, and workshops are void of any discussion of the MLM industry.

Ambulance-chasing attorneys are still out scouring the country for disgruntled ex-MLM distributors looking for a scapegoat for their failure. Class-action suits against MLM companies were at an all-time high around 1991 and 1992 (although this disturbing practice does seem to have peaked). The companies, knowing that bad news travels twice as fast and is 10 times more powerful than good news, and being acutely aware of the fickle, flighty nature of most MLM distributors, usually give in quickly. I call it gray mail.

This is a 47-year-old business with about 6 million distributors (not 15 million, as we are told). There were about 2.9 million in 1984. Our numbers have only slightly more than doubled in the last 12 years. What happened to geometric progression?

We keep hearing that there are more than 2,000 MLM companies in the United States (some claims go as high as 3,600 hundred). Even if you scrape the bottom of the barrel, you may come up with only 300 or 400. Less than half of these are more than a year old with a legitimate product or service. And indications are that the supply of opportunities is still far outstripping the demand.

We keep hearing that corporate America is discovering MLM and recognizing it as a more efficient way to move its products. If true, corporate America would be right. But I can count, on two hands and a toe, the major (previously non-MLM) corporations that have formally embraced and used the MLM concept within the last 15 years.

The proliferation of money-games, chain-letter schemes, downline building services, feeder programs, and, yes, even pyramid and Ponzi schemes seems to be at an all-time high. Not only is the industry not effectively policing these schemes, it is endorsing and promoting them! Sure, the trade publications print the ads, but the publications are not the guilty parties here. It's not their job to be judge and jury. It's ours! If it looks like a skunk and smells like a skunk . . . don't take it home for a pet!

The interest that distributors seem to take in the industry as a whole is underwhelming. Several very good, strictly informative, educational publications are available to all network marketers. These publications are subscription-based and exist only to serve the industry in general. It's pathetic that the circulation of

> **I**f it looks like a skunk and smells like a skunk . . . don't take it home for a pet!

all these publications combined doesn't even make up 0.1% (literally) of those that have been in MLM since they began publishing.

Please understand that I don't intend to put down MLM. I am an advocate of this industry, and I dearly love it. That's why this disturbs me so much. It's like watching a sick friend who has been treated by a bogus faith healer. If you think you're cured, you won't search for a cure. MLM is still a damaged product and, until we realize it, no one is going to try to repair it.

For those of you who are looking into MLM, please don't be dissuaded from joining by these comments. Numerous opportunities still exist that exemplify everything that is good about network marketing. I cannot emphasize enough that this industry has a very positive, bright side as well. It's just not the focus of this discussion. This article is directed more to those already in MLM. It's a wake-up call, a kick in the butt. Big Brother (federal regulation) is coming, so we better get our act together before they throw the baby out with the bath water (let us not forget, Congress came within 11 votes of doing just that when it came to the franchise industry back in 1963). Historically speaking, this could still mean it's a few years away, but we've got a few years' work ahead of us. Personally, I think we can fix it—and before the end of the decade—but first we must acknowledge that it's broken!

I know this article will step on the toes of some companies and many upline leaders who have disseminated this "industry of the '90s" propaganda. These leaders are not to blame either. They're doing their jobs. Encouraging and motivating is part of a good leader's responsibility, and damage control is the company's job. These leaders would be inept in their duties if they didn't try to paint as rosy a picture as possible of MLM to their people. This isn't about blame; it's about the truth. It's about making things better.

Besides, who can blame them? With the state of the economy the way it is, with more than 5 million people losing their jobs in the last 10 years, and with all the advantages MLM has to offer this country, it is rather unbelievable that MLM hasn't "exploded" like we keep hearing it has.

The responsibility to communicate the true state of the MLM industry lies with watchdogs and advocates such as myself. It's our job to discover and relate both the positive and the negative, to take the blinders off, if just for a moment, so no one gets blindsided.

John F. Kennedy said, "Ask not what your country can do for you, ask what you can do for your country." He understood that the more we do for our country, the more our country can offer us. It's no different in MLM.

You can't just sit around complaining about how MLM isn't working for you if you're not working for it.

We can do some very inexpensive, simple things to support the industry as a whole. If only a fraction of us followed through, MLM could still easily become the industry of the '90s!

## *Discussion*

This article coincided with a major MLM trade publication dropping my column. The editor claimed my articles were becoming too negative, and that their publication was a "very positive, upbeat publication." In other words, their advertisers would get upset.

I sent this article with a personal letter challenging various other MLM trade publications to run it. Remarkably, three agreed they would, and two actually had the guts to follow through. Of course, one was sandwiched in between a promotion for a new trade organization they were supporting (which they claimed my article demonstrated the need for), but nonetheless, they got the message out. That's what counts.

The response? 99% positive! And the other 1% didn't like a word of it but could never rebut any particular point. They just—didn't like it.

So, did MLM ever become the "industry of the '90s?" Well, it certainly got bigger as far as participants, number of opportunities, and sales volume, but no, it didn't live up to its promise. Not at all. In fact, in some ways we've gone a little backward. As discussed in more detail later, the hype in this business is far worse that it's ever been. Although we've certainly made some progress in getting positive media attention, for the most part we'll about as ignored as we were in 1993.

Maybe, at least for now, it's for the best.

Ah, but surely we're going to be the "industry of the '00s"!

\* \* \*

A few months earlier, while in a much happier state of mind and in an effort to disprove the notion that I was "too serious" and had no sense of humor, I wrote the following article. It came from an idea I had while I was driving home and passed a construction site just outside of town. As I passed the naked steel girders of what would soon be our new Kaiser hospital, a question suddenly came to mind. It happened without forethought, almost instantaneously. I

asked myself, Why do they say a building that's under construction is being "built," but a structure that's completed is
a "building?" Shouldn't if be the other way around?

This wasn't the first time I'd asked myself such a rhetor-
ical question. For example:

Why is it that when you transport something by car it's
called a shipment, but when you transport it by ship it's
called cargo?

Why do all dictionaries contain a definition for the
word *dictionary?* Why don't they just say: dic•tio•nary
('dik-sh∂-"ner-E) noun 1. This thing you're reading!

And for that matter, why isn't the word *phonetic* spelled
the way it sounds?

Why are there instructions on a bottle of shampoo? Are
there really people out there who massage in the shampoo—then wet their hair?

Why do the little bags of peanuts the airlines give you
have instructions on them at all? In fact, they do! It says: Open
bag, eat nuts. I'd hate to screw that up and do it backward.

Why does the mashed potatoes section of a TV dinner
always take three times longer to cook in a microwave?

Why is the warning "Do not turn upside down" on
Tesco's Tiramisu dessert printed on the *bottom* of the box?
(It's true, I checked.)

Why does it say on a bottle of Nytol sleep aid, "*May*
cause drowsiness"? Do they not have a lot of confidence in
their product?

Why do hot dogs always come eight to a pack, but the
buns always come six to a pack? (I know that's an old one,
but it's still a good question.)

Why does the prison doctor who administers lethal injections dab the subject's arm with alcohol before inserting the needle (it's true!)? Is this guy really concerned about getting an infection?

Unfortunately for my loved ones, these episodes happen quite frequently. During one such attack in October 1992, I wrote the following article. Stay with it. There is an MLM connection eventually.

## *Why Is It . . . ?*

If it were possible to count all the words we speak within our lifetime, I'd guess *I* would be number one, *and* would be a distant second, closely followed by *to*. Unless you're me. Then you'd probably find *why* right on *I*'s tail. Ever since I was a small child, I've been asking that question.

I remember vividly having the "birds and the bees" explained to me at a very early age because I asked why Mommy had to go all the way to the hospital for my baby brother if the doctor was going to deliver him. After Dad did the honors of telling me the real story right from the start (he knew there was no hope of me ever buying into the stork bit), I remember asking why, after this elaborate, very deliberate, incredibly meaningful event between a man and a woman, did the father always

> I remember vividly having the "birds and the bees" explained to me at a very early age because I asked why Mommy had to go all the way to the hospital for my baby brother if the doctor was going to deliver him.

act surprised when told his wife was expecting. Did he forget?

About the age of nine or ten, during a cross-country trip, I asked my parents, "Why do they say we drive on a parkway and park on a driveway?" Not until many years later did I hear, to my astonishment, that very same question asked of millions of television viewers during a show by the comedian Gallagher.

Gallagher has always been one of my favorite comics. He asks a lot of good *why* questions. Why is there an expiration date on sour cream? Why don't bomb and comb rhyme (a variation of my own question about do and go)? Why is there a permanent press setting on an iron? I love this guy!

I know that taking this why thing too far can get obnoxious. I've really had to struggle to not ask the vendors at Oakland A's games why their catsup containers are yellow and their mustard containers are red. That makes no sense. I've been dying to ask one of the tellers at my local bank why the bank just installed Braille instructions on the drive-up automatic teller machine. I don't know how much longer I can last on that one, but I'm hanging in there.

Why would anyone buy Levi's oversized jeans? Why don't they just buy normal jeans a couple sizes too big?

Why do fat chance and slim chance mean the same thing?

Why do all Bic lighters carry a warning label informing you the contents are *flammable*. Isn't that why you bought it? To make fire?

Why does that same warning label suggest that the user should "not hold flame near face"? Who is this warning for, the Marlboro Man . . . or Cro-Magnon Man?

Why did kamikaze pilots wear helmets? To prevent head injury?

What time is it at the North Pole? (I know that's not a *why* question, but it's still a darn good one. Think about it.)

This insatiable appetite to know why has carried into my research and observation of the network marketing industry as well. For example, why is it that if a large conventional business, employing thousands of people, goes bankrupt or is on the verge of closing, its employees, and many times the company itself, are pitied and people root for the company to survive? But if an MLM company, employing just as many honest, hard-working people shuts down, it's a scam? Every time.

Why do ex-employees of closed companies usually see themselves as unlucky, or victims of the economy, whereas ex-distributors for closed MLMs consider themselves "ripped off," or victims of the company, or the MLM concept?

Along the same lines, why is it that if a car, real estate, or insurance salesperson fails, he or she just wasn't a good salesperson? But if an MLM distributor fails, it wasn't a good product, company, or compensation plan?

Why is it that if you create a company hierarchy where all those at the bottom can only succeed by climbing over those above them, and those above are doing everything they can to make sure that those below stay below, this is considered a legal, legitimate pursuit of the free enterprise system? If, however, you create the exact same hierarchy, but allow those at the bottom to create, and be at the top of, their own hierarchies, with unlimited support, training, and encouragement from all those above them, this is considered a pyramid scheme?

Why is it that many states conduct lotteries that take in tens of millions of dollars more than they pay out—mostly from the middle and lower class—which have a 1-in-10 million chance of winning, but these same states will investigate, file suit, and even shut down some MLM opportunities because their compensation plan employs a "luck factor"?

Why are network marketing companies attacked and heavily fined by either the FTC or FDA due to vague, indirect insinuations that their product might be effective in preventing or treating an ailment, but numerous high-profile religious icons, nightly on national television in front of millions of viewers, can claim to immediately and completely eliminate every disease known to science by a simple touch of the hand—and nobody says a word?

Why is it that in any other kind of business that involves sales it's generally considered shady or deceptive if your potential employer does not tell you what the top earners are making and what the maximum potential of the commission structure is, but only in network marketing do state and federal authorities consider it shady or deceptive if you *do* provide this information?

I want to clarify something about that last question. I'm not an advocate of high earnings claims in MLM. But nonetheless, it infuriates me to hear stories of top distributors being prosecuted for displaying evidence of their incomes, even with a stern disclaimer, and proof that the stated income is factual. Prosecuted for telling the truth!

Why ask why?

Sometimes for fun, and sometimes—to know the answer!

## Discussion

I can summarize every pitch ever given by every network marketer who has ever given one: "We have the highest quality products that sell themselves . . . a great, duplicatable support system . . . the most lucrative compensation plan in the industry . . . and our company is debt free, financially strong, and about to go into momentum!" Right? Isn't that what *everyone* basically has told you about the deal they want you to join? Well, when someone says this stuff to you, ask them "How do you *know*?" In other words, don't let them tell you what the script says, or what they were taught to say, or what they think you want to hear—find out how they know all these things are true. Are they just telling you what they think you need to hear to get you enrolled, or can they validate their claims? Are there *reasons* behind them?

There is a huge difference between *believing* something and *knowing* something. To believe that your opportunity has the most lucrative compensation plan, or the best products, or the most financially stable company, is great—but it's not the same as *knowing* it. And this will come through in your presentation.

When you believe something, you recognize that while

**T**here is a huge difference between *believing* something and *knowing* something.

it may or may not be true, you just personally believe it is. When you know something, you *know* it. There is no question.

For example, I personally believe there was no second gunman on the grassy knoll, but there was a conspiracy in the assassination of John Kennedy. I accept the fact that there is evidence to the contrary on both counts, and I may be wrong. I just don't believe I am. Now, if I had been standing in Daley Plaza back in 1963 and had been looking up at the grassy knoll at the time the shots were fired and no one was standing there, then I would no longer believe there was no gunman there—I would absolutely know it!

Asking why, or any type of question (who, when, where) allows you to gain knowledge about your opportunity. The more you know, the more you *know.*

\* \* \*

MLM has become a real dog-eat-dog world. There is so much competition for distributors nowadays that many of them will say or do whatever they have to say to recruit a prospect away from someone else. It reminds me of the old cliché scene where two women are fighting over a bargain at the dress counter, only to have the dress rip in half as each tries to pull it free from the other. That's exactly what a lot of distributors are doing to MLM right now.

My *MarketWave* newsletter used to review and rate MLM opportunities (before I became a full-time distributor, thus creating an obvious conflict of interest). I had a voice-mail system tied to an 800 number so people could request samples of the publication or just leave me a message. This line turned into a kind of feedback line for my subscribers or whoever else felt compelled to comment on something I'd written. This is also where I got the majority of those cowardly, anonymous messages. In *MarketWave*, my reviews were divided into five categories, each receiving a grade of A, B, C, D, or F. A grade-point average concluded each opportunity review. Inevitably, each positive review resulting in a high grade was followed by messages and letters from distributors for competing opportunities suggesting I "cut down on the hard drugs," as one put it, or otherwise give up on the MLM analysis business because I "don't have a clue." Many went so far as to explain all the reasons why that other MLM opportunity, why every other opportunity for that matter, should be a D+ at best.

Today, this internal MLM bashing appears to be increasing to a fever pitch. The result was the following article.

## The MLM Stigma: Are We Our Own Worst Enemies?

HAVE YOU EVER lived next door to a couple who fought every single night? Night after night? She's screaming, he's cursing, the kids are crying, dishes are breaking, sirens approach in the distance. . . . How would you feel about this couple the next morning, as you passed them on your way to the bus stop? No matter how pleasant and polite they were to you in person, what would your gut reaction be?

What if a business associate from a competing firm approached you to work for his company? The company has 10 divisions, he tells you, and the other nine, besides the one he's in charge of, are all run by incompetent lunatics. They're crooked, they are producing few benefits to the company, their sales are down, and many will probably be canned before month's end. "But it's a great company!" he exclaims. "You've just got to come to work for me."

Dan Democrat is on TV discussing all the improprieties of Rick Republican. Rick accepted big-time contributions from the oil industry, Dan states, on the record, then vetoed a series of clean air bills. Why, he also appointed his brother-in-law to a high-ranking government position. Dan is also quick to point out that Rick wrote more bum checks than anybody in Congress!

Of course, Rick is on the radio, being interviewed about his recent accusation that Dan drank half a beer when he was 10 (Dan claims he didn't swallow it, but still . . .). Oh, and Dan also had the highest absentee rate of any congressman in his state, and let's not forget that racial remark he made back in 1974 (he told an Italian joke at a dinner party) or that trip he took to Orlando with the kids, on taxpayer money!

Then there's poor ol' Ernest Honest. Senator from Anystate USA. He's worked hard through these many years and has served his constituents to the best of his ability. Never missed a day of work, never took a bribe, always listened to the people—and just can't figure out why they all so easily assume every politician is a dishonest, self-serving crook.

Are you getting the analogies here? Does any of this sound familiar? Let me be more specific.

Many MLM distributors in this country have a nasty habit of putting down, sometimes with vile excess, any MLM opportunity that is not theirs! Then we all stand around wondering why everyone has such a bad attitude about MLM.

I know this phenomenon all too well. Literally every negative review I published in *MarketWave* was inevitably met with praise by those not involved with that opportunity. If the review was positive, criticism by competing distributors would sometimes fill up my voice-mail box. And some of it gets downright ugly.

A classic example of this was an anonymous message I received from an individual who took me to task for reviewing such companies as "Nu Scam, Scamway, Matol the Throw Up Liquid, Nasty Safety Associates," etc. This rather pompous individual informed me he was pleased I was promoting these larger, "saturated" companies and leaving the "little companies for the good people." Obviously, I could go for days discussing the flaws in this person's logic and understanding of this industry and my publication (if only little companies have "good people," won't they someday be big companies too?).

And the sad part is, I get dozens of these cowardly, ignorant, anonymous little barbs every month. So many people in this industry will rip into the competition whenever possible, even if it's unprovoked!

How many times have you heard about what those other guys put into their skin cream, or what a rip-off somebody's marketing plan is, or how so-and-so is going out of business (even if they're not), or the checkered past of its president. Think about it. Ask any distributor for an MLM company what he thinks of another MLM company. Tell him you're considering getting involved with that other company, and you'll really get the dirt.

So why does this happen? I believe there are two primary reasons. First, unlike conventional business, all MLM companies are in competition with each other, even if one sells cosmetics and the other sells automotive products. They all have one product in common—the opportunity. Second, a person willing to consider an MLM opportunity is still considered a rare commodity. Once you're exposed as being receptive to MLM (usually by joining it), you become fair game. You become the life's blood of someone's organization and potentially of someone else's.

The first step in combating the media's naiveté, and regulatory agency ignorance, is to get our own act together. We have to understand that we are still a small, vulnerable, but growing little club, which desperately needs to become united for the challenging times just ahead.

We also have to realize that our opportunity isn't the only good opportunity. Accept that there just might be one or two (or 20 or 50) others that are legitimate and worthwhile. When one of your MLM brothers or sisters tells you he or she is in that other opportunity, don't smirk and exclaim, "But their products suck. Here, try ours!" Instead, give them a thumbs up and say, "Congratulations!"

What if every MLM participant made a point of buying all their goods and services from other MLM companies? Let's face it. Your company isn't the only one with great products either. Some really wonderful stuff is in the

MLM marketplace, but most people will never experience it—because they would be supporting the "competition."

Nobody knows for sure how many MLM opportunities there are in the United States. I estimate as many as 800. Others claim to have verified the existence of as many as 1,200. When you suggest that your opportunity is the only legitimate one, you malign the other 1,199 and thus the entire industry.

And don't think for a second that people outside our little home called MLM don't hear the dishes breaking.

## Discussion

I was recently asked for my choices of the top 20 MLM opportunities in the United States today as part of a survey for *Network Marketing Today* magazine. Quite frankly, I had a hard time coming up with more than eight that I really, really liked. Twenty that I would consider at least recommendable was no problem. A list of 40 that I would not recommend against would even be possible for me, perhaps even 50 if I tried hard.

Of course, this was all based on my personal opinion, and I'm a bit on the picky side. Granted, that's still a minority of all the opportunities available—but it's a lot more than one!

And it only takes one to be successful.

\* \* \*

Three groups are actually responsible for perpetuating the MLM stigma. The distributors themselves are only one. Certain regulatory bodies within state and federal government are the second (to be discussed in a moment). The

third, quite obviously, is the media. I believe the media—
that being print, radio, and, most important, television—is
the most important group in our challenge to gain
respectability and widespread public acceptance. How can
that be accomplished? Why isn't it happening already?
When will it happen? All good questions, and the ones I
addressed in the next article.

## MLM Bashing in the Media: Why It May Never End and What We Can Do About It!

YOU MAY HAVE noticed that a kind of stigma surrounds
multilevel marketing in this country. Kind of? Heck, most
people outside the industry who are aware of it think this
form of business is nothing but scams, schemes, and illegal
pyramids. If you were to listen only to the tabloid TV shows
(such as the trashing of Amway on *American Journal* or
Kalo Vita on *PrimeTime Live*) or even the more "reputable"
news programs (such as *Nightline*'s embarrassing attempt at
an exposé of NuSkin back in 1992), you'd quickly get the
impression we are nothing but a bunch of cults. Only we
sacrifice paychecks instead of animals.

Although that certainly doesn't apply to everyone out
there, unfortunately it does seem that about every television
producer and newspaper columnist believes this myth
about MLM. Or do they?

Considering all the advantages to starting an MLM distributorship over a conventional business, not the least of
which is a significantly reduced financial risk, I've got to

believe these media people have more of a clue about what's good about MLM than they're letting on. But let's face it—bad news sells. When was the last time you saw *20/20* or *60 Minutes* do a piece on how MLM made someone wealthy or saved them from bankruptcy, or how wonderful many of the products are?

The aforementioned Amway segment is a great example. What do you suppose would have happened if these journalists from *American Journal* had brought their camera crew into a low-key, professionally run Amway training meeting? If there were no clown on stage claiming he'd rather leave his wife than his Amway business, but, rather, a soft-spoken professional trainer giving a dignified business presentation—would it have aired? Of course not! And if you're smiling right now at the idea that such a presentation would exist in Amway, or any MLM opportunity, then you are buying into the same propaganda. They do exist, you just don't hear about them. They're not newsworthy!

Sure, *60 Minutes* also aired exposés on companies like International Heritage and Equinox, which were, in my opinion, both worthy targets. But, what about all the wonderful success stories? What about all the good, honest, MLM companies that are changing thousands of people's lives for the better? Good MLMers being depicted on TV are about as rare as good men. Imagine turning on your TV one afternoon and hearing this: "Monogamous men who respect their wives, take care of their families, and work hard at their jobs—next, on Oprah."

It'll never happen. We want the dirt!

Word-of-mouth is the most powerful form of advertising and promotion the world has ever seen. But if we continue to rely on "networking" to end this nasty reputation we have and to gain acceptance and respect from the masses, we're wasting our breath. For every one of us out there saying nice things about MLM, there are 10 slamming it to death. Let's face it, bad news not only travels twice as fast as good news and is 10 times more powerful, but the news tends to get worse with each person down the line. And consider this: If something good happens to your opportunity, who passes the good news along? Those in your opportunity. What if a rumor starts that your company is having financial problems? That's right, every MLMer in the country knows about it! And eventually, if the news is bad enough to make it to national television or the wire services, the whole country hears the bad news.

But the challenge we face with MLM bashing in the media goes deeper than just a thirst for dirt. I think it gets even dirtier.

How does the news media make its money? Think about it: Radio, television, magazines, and newspapers all live and die on advertising dollars! No advertising, no *USA Today*. No commercials, no *Nightline*. How do you think these "powers that be" feel about an industry that doesn't advertise?

What if MLM were to get as big as franchising, which is certainly a possibility someday. Do you think the media might be a tad concerned about more than one-third of all the goods and services in this country being moved by word-of-mouth alone? That's a 33% reduction in ad revenue!

Now, I'm not going so far as to suggest that some kind of monumental conspiracy against MLM exists. Moving only about 1.5% of all goods and services doesn't make us that much of a threat—yet. This is why the bashing may never stop in the future. The bigger we get, the more effort they'll spend to make sure we stay small.

Right now, our lack of mainstream advertising is only creating a lack of incentive for the media to lay off. If Amway were a regular million-dollar sponsor of *American Journal*, it wouldn't have been featured negatively even if the show had discovered that Jay Van Andel or Rich DeVos was the second gunman on the grassy knoll!

Burke Hedges cites another great example in his best-selling book *Who Stole The American Dream?* When *USA Today* joined the foray in railroading NuSkin in 1992, he pointed out that NuSkin (which he doesn't mention by name) was then forced to pay $120,000 for two full-page ads to tell NuSkin's side of the story. It seems like the media is determined to get our advertising dollars one way or the other, doesn't it?

> If Amway were a regular million-dollar sponsor of *American Journal*, it wouldn't have been featured negatively even if the show had discovered that Jay Van Andel or Rich DeVos was the second gunman on the grassy knoll!

This is where we've got to start. These are the avenues we must use to put a positive image of our industry out to the masses. It still amazes me how much credibility the media has with the American public. You and I could pitch

MLM to a prospect until we grow old and never get anywhere, but if people hear Larry King say they should check
it out, they're at the next opportunity meeting with open
ears! (And no, Larry King never said any such thing, so
don't start any rumors—he was just an example.)

I don't suggest we try to change the opinions or actions
of the networks or newspapers. We can't fight the power of
the almighty buck. What I'm suggesting is that this industry must find a way to buy the time on television and radio,
and the space in the newspapers, and present the other side
of the story ourselves. If we wait for the media to do it on
its own, no MLM herbal/amino acid product in the world
will keep us alive long enough to see it happen.

So, who's going to do it?

Few companies will. Most MLM operations don't have
advertising budgets, remember?

No MLM support organization is going to. Most I
know are having enough trouble paying rent on their
offices, let alone paying for a 60-second spot on national
TV.

No trade organization is going to. The Direct Selling
Association still doesn't seem to take MLM seriously
enough, and our two MLM-specific trade organizations are
years away from achieving the financial means to pull this
off effectively.

A wealthy distributor? You've got to be kidding.

An MLM publication? Trust me—no chance.

A generic lead-generation service? It's possible, but I'm
no longer confident there's one committed enough to take
it this far.

Hmmmm. Who's left?

It's us! It's you and me. The seven-and-some-odd million of us who really need to have this media-created veil lifted from the faces of the masses.

I wrote a column a few months back called "Crazy Ideas That Just Might Save MLM" (which does not appear in this book). Well, here's another one. How about one of our trade organizations, or even an alliance of MLM companies, creating a massive distributor ad co-op? It would have to be primarily distributor funded, with the companies only promoting it. Of course, even without an advertising budget, some companies could also contribute, assuming they'd be willing to cut back on a few $20,000 per day guest speakers at their conventions.

If enough companies and distributors participated, we could make some monumental progress in a very short time. Just imagine. Not only would we be presenting a truer, positive, more realistic image of network marketing, but all the media heads would suddenly see network marketing as a major source of revenue!

Just think of all the nice things they'd say about us if we helped pay their salaries!

## Discussion

I recently read an article in *Good Housekeeping* magazine that attempted to educate its readers on how to separate the "real opportunities from the scams." While I admire and respect the writer's attempt to expose the hype and empty promises heaped on prospects by some MLM distributors, the article was a classic example of the very skewed and biased perspective many mainstream writers have toward MLM.

For example, the article contains a story of a man who spent a year (and a great deal of time and money) building his MLM business, only to net $18.64. This was presented as an example of MLM's "empty promises." But let's put this in perspective. Had this been any other form of business endeavor, a first-year net profit of any amount would have been considered a major success story! Most conventional business start-ups don't ever turn a profit at all, and the successful ones usually only do so in their second or third year, meanwhile losing thousands of dollars. Only in MLM is breaking even in your first year considered a major failing.

The writer also dredges up the old, tired argument that less than 2% of those who attempt an MLM business ever make a substantial income from it. Of course, thousands make a nice, moderate living, and tens of thousands achieve their goal of a small supplemental income of a few hundred dollars—but for some reason, this doesn't seem to count. Only great wealth is viewed as "success" by most mainstream media critics.

And, once again, a statistic considered par for the course in any other pursuit is strangely considered a sign of inadequacy when applied to just network marketing. After all, less than 2% of all those who attempt a legal career ever pass the bar exam. Less than 2% of those who attempt a political career ever get elected to any office. Less than 2% of those who pursue a professional baseball career ever make it to the major leagues. And, of course, less than 2% of those who attempt *any* kind of business venture ever make any money at all from it. In fact, I'd guess that less than 2% of all those who pursue a job as a staff writer for a national magazine ever succeed. So, should we all just crawl in a hole somewhere and never attempt to succeed at anything?

Besides, the reason 98% fail to make any substantial income from MLM is because *most* of them don't do what they're suppose to do to succeed. It's kind of like this: Let's say a company was going to test a new pain reliever. They hand a sample of the product to 10 people with a headache. Five throw it in a drawer and never touch it again. Four fondle it a little, smell it, maybe break off a little tiny piece and take it, but that's about it. Only one actually consumes the sample. When polled, nine claim they still have a headache, and one experiences complete relief. A magazine editor then writes an article claiming, "Only 10% of those who were given the product experienced any relief from their headache." Would this be a fair criticism? Of course not.

Since my "MLM Bashing in the Media" article was written, I've come up with a couple of other angles to consider. Rather than trying to conjure up advertising funds to appease the media (which really smacks of protection money if you really think about it), why not go all the way and get some key media people involved in the industry itself? One major mainstream business publication has already taken this step, and lo and behold, it is now one of the industry's biggest supporters.

That same publication, the more than a century old *Success* magazine, ran a very positive (almost to a fault) feature on network marketing back in March 1992. That issue broke their all-time single-issue sales record by a substantial margin (and probably increased the revenue of self-service copy centers by a goodly sum as well). Considering the reaction of the industry to this feature, it amazes me that so few other newsstand business publications have followed suit. Recent articles (mostly very positive) in *The Wall Street Journal, The New York Times, Entrepreneur, Home Business,* and *Income Opportunities* have also been hoarded by credibility-starved MLM distributors looking for reputable and fairly presented reporting on network marketing. I believe the mainstream media is just beginning to discover that a lot of MLM distributor money is available, and all the media has to do to tap into it is present our industry fairly and truthfully.

There are now nationally distributed newsstand magazines devoted almost entirely to network and direct marketing (such as *Network Marketing Lifestyles, Opportunity World,* and *Wealth Building*). Although I doubt the combined circulation of all of these publications exceeds that of *Forbes* or *Inc.,* it's still positive mainstream exposure that we've never gotten before and it's gotta help.

There's a radio station in Santa Cruz, California, that figured out how to make money in MLM. Instead of selling the air time to a certain on-air personality, they enrolled in his MLM company as a distributor, then let him pitch his products during his daily live program. After about a year that station was earning many times what the air time would have sold for, and the show has now been syndicated to over 200 other stations. Imagine what would happen if this same concept were adapted to television! Give it time. It'll happen.

So there are two other angles we should look at. Get some revenue to the media heads via overrides like the rest of us, or simply sell out every issue that features a fair and balanced depiction of our industry.

When the national media figures out how to make big bucks from MLM, we *will* be the industry of the '00s!

\* \* \*

Immediately following the last article, I approached the subject of the third and final group responsible for the persistent negative image of MLM—state and federal regulators.

# Government Scrutiny of Network Marketing

FEDERAL AND STATE regulators, such as your postal inspector, attorney generals, the Federal Trade Commission, and the Securities and Exchange Commission, exist primarily, if not in some cases solely, to protect us all. In most cases, they do a bang-up job, and for that we should thank them.

When it comes specifically to network marketing, however, their performance, at least in many cases, has been less than admirable.

As a result of budget cuts, many state consumer fraud and consumer protection departments are manned by only skeleton crews, and I've heard that a few states have even had no staff at all! The phones just ring all day (I think I've called a few of those states recently). Of course, one way for these agencies to demonstrate their value and effectiveness (and maintain their funding) is to close down a bunch of those "pyramid schemes." You know, those deals that have pyramid-shaped downlines.

Unfortunately, few federal and state regulators truly understand multilevel marketing. Just the fact that our organizations are thought of as being pyramidal in shape is a classic example. Our organizations are in fact diamond-shaped, where the levels with the most distributors are always somewhere in the middle. The typical corporate structure is a perfect pyramid. The church and family hierarchies are pyramid shaped. And yes, the hierarchy of the state and federal government is shaped like a pyramid!

So the double irony here is that not only are the attackers of some MLM programs operating a pyramid-based organization themselves, but . . . multilevel marketing is actually the only form of business that does not form a pyramid!

Another example of the confusion that exists among many regulators is a discussion I recently had with an inspector from the Michigan attorney general's (AG) office. He informed me that "personal consumption does not satisfy the 70% rule" in that state. In other words, all distributors must retail 70% of their last order to satisfy this legal requirement, or else the program would be illegal. Obviously, this means that right now about 99% of all MLM companies in the country are illegal in the state of Michigan!

**M**ultilevel marketing is actually the only form of business that does not form a pyramid!

Why does this expose confusion? Think about it. Michigan

is declaring that if your company allows you to only purchase a small, harmless amount of product for your personal consumption, your company is doing something wrong. If, however, your company requires you to purchase 2.3 times the amount you can use yourself (30% for you, 70% to sell), at 2.3 times the cost, that's okay.

Michigan feels that those MLM programs in which the majority of your customers are the distributors themselves are those in which you are thus financially rewarded for the act of recruiting (a distinguishing element of a pyramid scheme). This is an arguable point, I agree. If I were an attorney general, I would want to err on whatever side involved the least financial risk for the distributor. Besides, wholesale buying clubs are perfectly legal. Why shouldn't they be network marketed?

Other states have also invoked this 70% retail rule. First question: How many times have distributors been hurt by buying more product than they can use or sell? Answer: Tens of thousands. Next question: How many have been hurt by buying only what they can comfortably consume themselves? Answer: None. Last question: Isn't it the job of these agencies to prevent people from getting hurt?

In my conversations over the years with various regulators I have found that a prejudice toward MLM pervades many of these agencies. Prejudice means to prejudge. Many regulators do seem to have a negative attitude toward MLM operations going into an investigation. I remember speaking to a Florida AG investigator back in 1991 regarding an upcoming investigation of a large, prominent MLM company. He likened their distributors to "a bunch of lemmings running around duplicating each other." I'll bet that company received a very fair and nonbiased evaluation, don't you think?

Let's move on to what I believe may be one of the greatest injustices and abuses of our industry—using MLM companies as free publicity, as a way of getting an elected regulator, senator, or congressman in front of the electorate, in a positive light, for the purpose of public recognition—and thus their votes.

Maybe I'm being paranoid, but tell me if there is a peculiar pattern forming here.

Let's go back to 1971. Two of the most prominent MLM operations then were Culture Farms and Holiday Magic (by most prominent I mean getting the most attention, not necessarily largest or oldest). The two MLM operations that received the most regulatory attack around that time were Holiday Magic and Culture Farms. In fact, they were both eventually closed down for being illegal pyramid schemes.

In 1975, Amway was really beginning to take off and could easily be considered the "most prominent" company of that year. That same year, the FTC filed charges against Amway accusing it of being an illegal pyramid. Not until 4 years later did Amway win the right to exist, and a legal precedent was formed that distinguished between illegal pyramids and legal multilevel operations.

In 1983, Herbalife really exploded and was unquestionably the most prominent MLM opportunity of that time. Beginning in late 1982 and throughout 1983, Herbalife came under perpetual attack by both state and federal regulators, culminating in a senate subcommittee hearing in 1984.

Arguably the most prominent MLM operation of 1987 was National Safety Associates (NSA). The mid to late 1980s were NSA's prime years, and the first actions were taken against it in 1987, peaking in 1991 with actions filed by 10 states.

Picking the most prominent MLM company of 1991 is a slam dunk. NuSkin began one of the most momentous growth phases ever witnessed in the history of MLM during that year. It also got one of the worst regulatory beatings as well (which the media was quick to pick up on, of course). The genesis of the NuSkin attack seems to be, once again, the state of Michigan, whose attorney general was allowed to punch away at it practically unimpeded in front of a national *Nightline* audience of millions. He was, by the way, reelected the following year.

If you haven't figured out the pattern yet, that last line was a big hint. The most important year in a campaign for reelection is not the year of the election; it's the previous year. That's when the candidate really needs to build his reputation, recognition, and credibility. It's the year going into the primaries. Notice that in every preelection year other than 1979, whichever MLM company was the most prominent was also the most attacked!

Coincidence? Maybe.

Why not 1979, then, you might be asking. Well, that was the year of the final Amway decision, remember? That would have been, politically speaking, one of the worst years to attack an MLM company based on its legality or legitimacy.

It has been suggested by some old-time MLMers that I might be stretching it a bit by going back as far as 1971. But the real test is going to be what happens here in 1995. If my theory holds true, you won't want to be the most prominent company out there. This year you'll start seeing MLM companies advertising the fact that they're *not* going into momentum, or that they are not the fastest growing company in history. You may even see distributors having conversations like this:

**In every preelection year other than 1979, whichever MLM company was the most prominent was also the most attacked!**

"Hey, you guys said you were the 'premier' MLM opportunity!"

"Yeah, but you said you were 'exploding across North America!'"

"We're not exploding. You're exploding!"

"Get out of here. People are joining *your* company in droves."

"No way. They're all joining your company!"

But seriously, it will be very interesting to see what happens to the most prominent companies this year. If you think your company is going to be one of them, better make sure it's squeaky clean.

Of course, we all think our company is going to be the biggest, hottest deal around, don't we? I wonder what all the elected regulators would do if we all made our programs squeaky clean?

## Discussion

Several states are actually considered to be very MLM friendly, such as Oklahoma, Utah, New Mexico, and Arizona. I've had a couple good experiences with the AG's office of Washington since this article was written as well (it was the first time I ever heard an attorney general laugh. Yes, they are human!). Others have shown signs of some open-mindedness and discretion as well recently. And I shouldn't pick on Michigan so much. It seems to have the reputation as being the state where MLM companies go to die. Actually, I liken their attorney general's office to a hive of yellow jackets. They sting like crazy, but they rarely kill.

I had an interesting conversation with a representative of the Nevada AG's office recently. When I inquired as to the legality of a certain type of MLM plan, she began to lecture me on the difference between a "legal" MLM operation and a "pyramid." I already knew what she was telling me, but it was wonderful to hear nonetheless.

Of course, 1995 has come and gone since this article was written. Although three companies did experience significant growth and to varying degrees did come under scrutiny by some states, they managed to make it through unscathed. But a fourth, and potentially "most prominent" company, called Gold Unlimited, didn't even make it halfway through. Gold Unlimited claimed a distributor total of 94,000 by April (up from 20,000 just 4 months earlier). All state actions (and there were several) were dropped in June when postal authorities placed a federal restraining order on Gold Unlimited, thus finishing off what state regulators had already started. In 1999, we had two major hits. Early in the year there was an SEC action against International Heritage (who alleged to have more than 150,000 reps) and most recently an FTC action against Equinox (estimated more than 100,000 reps).

**O**r, how about just building the industry to a size where the total number of distributors constitutes a significant number of registered voters? We'll sure get some regulatory cooperation then—especially before election years!

Granted these companies may have been worthy targets (in my opinion), and I agree it is debatable whether the most-prominent-pre-election-year company curse kept its streak alive. Either way, 2003 should be a very interesting year.

Personally, I think government acceptance will happen as soon as they (or we) figure out what's in it for them. MLM programs are very popular fundraisers for charitable organizations and churches—why not political causes? And how about a network-marketed state lottery? Or, how about just building the industry to a size where the total number of distributors constitutes a significant number of registered voters? We'll sure get some regulatory cooperation then—especially before election years!

\* \* \*

If you're not totally bummed out by now, let me throw at you one more little essay I wrote, then I promise I'll lighten things up a bit. This next subject, however, I personally feel is the greatest challenge of all to this industry's long-term success and viability. It's not pretty, but it needs to be said.

## MLM Start-Ups: Are They Strangling the Industry?

IN ECONOMICS 101, they teach you about one of the most basic principles of economics—supply and demand. Here's a little economics lesson as it pertains to MLM. I promise I won't bore you.

In early 1991, I did a survey of MLM companies to try to determine the true number of MLM distributors in the United States. I came up with 6.1 million, and I counted a lot of people twice, I'm sure. In late 1995, I did another rough count and came up with 6.8 million, an 11.5% increase. The estimated number of MLM companies went from about 180 to 490, however. A 172% increase! The result? The average downline is 59% smaller today than it was 5 years ago.

For most of 1992 through early 1994, I offered my services as an MLM consultant, specializing in comp plan design. Most of my clients have been start-ups. I no longer offer that service, except for casual phone consultation. And even then, I play the role of devil's advocate almost exclusively. You see, I can no longer in good conscience support or assist people who are about to add more to the supply of MLM opportunities in an industry where the supply is already far outstripping the demand.

MLM veteran Art Meakin once suggested to me that the minimum number of distributors necessary to maintain an MLM operation on a base level (just keep it in business) was about 4,000. I concur with that number. In 1995, I was contacted by more than 150 potential clients looking to start up their own MLM operations. And, I'm not even close to being one of the major players in the MLM start-up consulting business. I expect the Alf Whites, Rod Cooks, Debbi Ballards, and Doris Woods of the industry are getting many times more business in this area than I am.

So it looks like, if I were to estimate that 400 companies will try to launch this year, I might be a bit conservative (quadruple that, maybe). So if those 400 companies need at least 4,000 distributors, they will need 1.6 million new distributors to join MLM this year just to barely survive. Let me put this in perspective.

Two thousand people are laid off from their jobs each day in this country. Even if that number were to double, and every single one of them were to join one of those 400 new MLM companies, every single day of the year, we would still need to find another 140,000 new distributors just to keep those companies in business—and that's not even counting what we'll need to replace all of those who leave the more than 600 existing companies—let alone allow them to grow.

It pains me to say this, but the estimated number of distributors in MLM was 6.5 million in 1993 and 1994, and there was "only" a 300,000 net increase in 1995. In fact, I suspect this industry may have suffered a slight net loss in 1994. Every year for the past several years, one or two major forces in MLM have successfully brought tons of fresh blood into the industry: NuSkin in 1991, Melaleuca in 1992, Quorum in 1993. And there were others.

But who in 1994 and 1995? A couple companies claimed huge numbers, but that's all they were—numbers. They had no distributor enrollment fees and absurd retail pricing (so customers would always become distributors) and rarely purged their inactive distributors. So their claims of more than 100,000 "distributors" could have more accurately described the number of "purchasers" in 1994. Still not bad, but based on the standard industry definition of "distributor" (those who at least have the intention of recruiting and retailing some amount of product), these companies actually brought in a fraction of what they have claimed.

Why didn't it happen? Why was there no blockbuster company in 1994 or 1995?

Instead, we saw several heavyweight MLM companies take major hits. Two or three of what I believed to be the best up-and-comers also stumbled (more like shot themselves in the foot, really).

Nope, 1994 was not a great year for MLM. Although 1995 was a decent sales year, it was only a moderate to poor growth year as far as active participants.

So . . . let's throw in another 400 companies and spread those 6.8 million distributors even thinner. That should help.

But seriously. What's the answer?

If it's done right, the rest of this decade has the potential to be one of the greatest periods in MLM history. September 1995 marked the 50th birthday of network marketing. Of course, our golden anniversary came and went with little fanfare, but still it's hard to deny that there must be something right about an industry that's survived for this long in spite of it all. Like franchising in the early 1960s, we've taken our lumps and come out better for the wear. With corporate downsizing and the massive migration toward home-based businesses (47 million as of December 1995, a 50% increase from 1989), what better timing could there be to expose the good side of this industry to the masses? Hopefully massive numbers of those masses will join us en masse. We're going to need them.

When I broached the subject of more tangible solutions in *MarketWave*, I suggested there should be some kind of regulation of the number of MLM companies, or at least some strenuous screening process. Or, how about requiring a $100,000 bond? That should take out the garbage. Imagine—if there were half as many companies, the average downline would be twice as big.

When I first made these suggestions, I caught some heat for being un-American. It was a restriction of free trade. Fine. You can restrict it and thrive, or expand it and dive. We could constitutionally right ourselves right out of a business.

But it'll never happen, of course. So it's a moot point. We will continue to see ads telling us to stop wasting our time with "penny-ante deals" and start our own MLM companies (because they "always make money") for as long as there are MLM publications that will take their money. And disgruntled, unsuccessful MLM distributors will continue to buy into the pitch and start MLM companies from their kitchen tables. And large numbers of MLM companies will continue to launch with no clue about what's required to be legally set up in all 50 states—thus operating illegally.

Why own an MLM company anyway? The whole beauty of network marketing was that you could start your own business without all the headaches and challenges faced by most conventional company owners. No payroll taxes, no legal hassles, no office to staff, no product development, and so on. As an MLM company owner, however, you not only have to perform all the same chores as any other company owner, but you have twice as much to worry about!

The typical employee-company relationship is one in which the employee relies on the company for his or her livelihood. Employees can't just pick up and leave and get another job anyplace they want. That's not the case in MLM. The company relies on the distributor! And most distributors know it. If things aren't perfect, your "employees" just might take one of those other 10 job offers they're getting every day. Imagine the pressure on the company.

If I did ever start my own company, it would have a full-blown computer system with all the bells and whistles in place from day one, a full stock of inventory of at least 25 quality products—and a million bucks in the bank!

One company that tried to launch recently didn't even have a computer. Management was keeping track of its company genealogy with a big chart on the wall. Seriously! And the names down by the baseboard were getting reeeeally small.

So what drives so many people, mainly ex-distributors, to want to start their own MLM companies? It can't be the income. Many network marketers make far more than the owners of their companies do. The income potential is at least equal. Perhaps it's the idea that nobody is doing it right and they can do it better. Everybody believes he or she can create the perfect MLM company. Well, there are 290 million people in this country, so unless you want to start up 290 million MLM companies, it isn't going to be perfect to everybody.

I think it's the illusion that it's so easy to start and run your own MLM company. Hey, just get some good software, whip up a few products, distributors run to you in droves, and you're rich!

Folks, do what I did. Before you ever decide to run your own MLM company, work out of the home office of one for just 1 month. The fantasy that this business is easy will be blasted from your mind with the force of a 20-megaton thermonuclear explosion.

Unfortunately, very few distributors ever really get to see the inside of an MLM operation.

And apparently even fewer of them took Economics 101.

## Discussion

Here's another crazy idea: How about adding another qualification to all compensation plans. To reach the highest position in the plan, the distributor must achieve some amount of group volume and personal volume and must have so many first-level distributors—and work at the home office for 30 days! What a great way to keep them from wandering off to start their own competing companies (not to mention keeping the overhead down in the one they're in).

And no, I'm not serious.

And yes, after the previous article was published I once again caught hell for even suggesting the idea of regulating the number of MLM companies. Frankly, I struggled with the idea myself. Being the card-carrying Libertarian that I am, I do feel it's a little paradoxical for me to advocate more governmental restrictions. The libertarian ideology, put simply, is that we essentially own ourselves, thus can do pretty much whatever we want to ourselves as long as no one else is harmed. Libertarians believe that government should be greatly downsized and there should be far fewer restrictions placed on its citizens (leaving those laws that detour us from harming others intact). I've reconciled (rationalized?) the two opposing philosophies by the firm belief that you *are* harming others by adding to an already grossly oversaturated market of opportunities.

This whole issue comes down to common business sense. It's simply a matter of what's best for the industry. Sure, everyone who wants to has a right to start an MLM company. We can't outlaw MLM start-ups (nor did I suggest we should), any more than we can outlaw poor business judgment. But I can certainly suggest that we not practice it!

Take a look at the streets of New York. There are more taxicabs than any other type of vehicle. That's why the number of hack licenses is regulated in that city. But, shouldn't anyone have the right to drive a cab in New York? Perhaps. But does it make any sense to allow even more cabs to flood this sea of yellow we call downtown New York? Of course not. To allow it is morally, logically, and financially unjustifiable. If you do allow it, you'll simply have more starving cab drivers.

This reminds me of a situation that occurred in San Francisco in the late 1980s. I was operating a computer business at the time, and a group of Economics 101 flunkies came into town and opened up a series of IBM clone shops, then proceeded to sell the units for what was undoubtedly below cost (I suppose their theory was to increase quantity and make up the difference on peripheral devices—I guess). The result was that most of the other dealers in the city were forced to drop their prices way down to stay competitive—so now everyone was selling just as many computers as they ever were, but now nobody was making any money!

Those I caught hell from after the previous article was published fall entirely into three categories: vendors of MLM software, publishers of MLM trade magazines who rely on MLM company advertising, and other consultants to start-up companies. I'm sure this is not a coincidence. Each of these groups has a direct financial interest in there being as many MLM companies as possible. It is also the primary reason why I have such a hard time really supporting our MLM trade organizations (although I do the best I can). I firmly believe this massive proliferation of MLM companies is the single greatest challenge facing this industry right now, yet our trade organizations are controlled by folks who fall into one or more of the previous three categories. In my opinion, this poses a tremendous conflict of interest.

One such consultant went so far as to write a rebuttal article to mine declaring the increased competition within the industry to be a very positive thing. She dismissed the idea of holding down the number of MLM programs as a fear-based reaction to this increase in "healthy competition."

Okay. So I suppose then that there would be no problem if *1 million* companies were to start up this year. Quite obviously, that would be utterly disastrous. So the question cannot possibly be whether there are too many MLM companies, but rather what number is too many? I thought we'd already surpassed it back when I wrote the previous article in 1995, and the situation is far worse today. My opponents seem to think we are, to this day, still well before it. This is one area where I would love to be wrong.

**I firmly believe this massive proliferation of MLM companies is the single greatest challenge facing this industry right now ...**

Has this increased competition increased the quality of opportunities? I suggest it has done exactly the opposite. After all, how do you compete for distributors? Simple. You offer them more in exchange for less. But what does that mean in MLM terms? It means you offer more income in exchange for less effort and money. And this overly competitive MLM marketplace has bred exactly that—a flood of fluff programs with token products that, for a small monthly purchase, will pay you the maximum possible commission. Is that good? Well, what do you gain with such an offer of great financial rewards with little effort? That's right. A downline full of people expecting great financial rewards who are putting forth little effort! And when they fail, guess who's going to get blamed?

Excess competition has also spurred rampant inflation within the network marketing industry. In an attempt to compete for distributors, companies have dramatically raised commission payouts over the last decade. The first multilevel compensation plan back in 1945 paid about 5% of total company wholesale revenue back to the field in commissions. Around 25% was typical during the 1960s and 1970s. Some companies achieved 35% total payouts in the 1980s. Today, actual payouts of 50% to 55% can be found with maximum potential payouts of more than 75%!

Is that good? Sure, if you can sell a 5.4 ounce bottle of shampoo for $27 *wholesale,* a prepaid calling card offering $1.25 per minute rates, or a $2.25 candy bar (all actual examples). Although competition tends to lower prices in conventional markets, it causes them to rise within network marketing because the only way to afford these higher commission payouts is to increase the margins on products (or just eat the profits).

Certainly not every MLM company has gone to the extreme of these worst-case examples I just mentioned. But most do have significantly higher pricing compared with like products found through conventional sources (stores, catalogs, and so forth). Yes, in some cases the "higher quality" justification is legitimate. Some phenomenal products can be found in this business. And yes, a few (very few) have kept their pricing comparable with the stores. But over all, this "competitive marketplace" seems to have brought product pricing to the brink of absurdity.

Also, again, the more opportunities there are, the smaller the average downline. When you keep slicing the pie into smaller and smaller pieces, we get less pie! Isn't that just common sense? And then, as there are fewer and fewer success stories, and more and more folks who are struggling and giving up, it gets even harder to bring in new blood. If the old adage "success breeds success" is true, then wouldn't the opposite be true?

If you're still not convinced, then let me update you on some numbers.

Based on an annual survey of MLM corporate software suppliers (conducted by a major industry trade publication), the number of companies that purchased such software (thus, the number who at least attempted to start an MLM operation) was over 700 in 1994, 950 in 1995, 1,350 in 1996, and 1,650 in 1997. That's not accumulative, that's *each year!* (And I rounded down to the nearest 50.) Yet, this same surveyor also conducted a phone audit and claimed to have verified the existence of 1,550 MLM companies in mid-1998 (a DSA survey pegged the number at about 700), and they were claiming there were over 2,000 MLM companies in 1994. I think there were more like 600 back then. So, in the *most optimistic* scenario (mine, believe it or not), that means we had a net gain of about 950 companies since the beginning of 1994 (or, a net gain of only 100 companies based on the DSA figures, or a 450 net *loss* based on the trade publication's figures). Thus, 3,700 out of over 4,650 didn't make it to their fourth birthday. That's at *least* an 80% failure rate.

It gets worse.

Surely many of those companies that were called as part of the phone audit were less than a year old, right? Some had probably just launched—and their lines were probably disconnected a few weeks later. What's more, I believe (and other more aware sources agree) it's possible that as many as half of all start-ups are not going to the major software houses, opting instead to hire an in-house programmer. Do you understand the implications of that? That means there could have been as many as *twice* the number of start-ups from 1994 through 1997. There *might* have been 8,350 failures out of 9,300! That would be a failure rate of . . . aaaggh, you do the math. I'm too depressed.

How about some good news? I spoke with two top MLM attorneys and got feedback from two of the top MLM software suppliers, and although my survey was an informal one, all agreed that the number of start-up clients was way down in 1998. Also, the number of mergers and acquisitions is rising, which is also positive. Anything that will compact the national distributor base under fewer companies will benefit the industry.

Yes, this is a free country based on free enterprise. You have the right to do whatever you legally need to do to compete, even if that means screwing it up for everybody else. Still . . . just because you have a right to do something doesn't always make it right!

\* \* \*

In late 1996 I wrote an article titled "The Hype Cycle." I suggested that if we could measure "hype" and then graph its occurrence, intensity, and duration, it would likely appear much like a sine wave—a wavy horizontal line intermittently dipping above and then below a certain median point. Each rise in the level of hype was followed by a sharp drop, usually due to some industry-shaking regulatory strike on a major MLM company. All the rats in the industry would then go away for a little while, leaving the

**J**ust because you have a right to do something doesn't always make it right!

rest of us to compete on a more level playing field. For a while. Slowly, eventually, once the heat was off and the smoke had cleared, they would creep their way back in. Until the next big hit, then the cycle would repeat.

When the article was written, this hype cycle created a very consistent pattern over the previous 20 years. Today, however, the hype quotient forms a line that just goes up . . . and up . . . and up. . . and up.

The following is an updated version of that article.

## The Hype Cycle Revs Up

So, WHAT IS "hype?" Messieurs Funk and Wagnalls define it accordingly: "To increase artificially; to deceive; to publicize extravagantly." Do many network marketers practice such activity? A loaded question, obviously. But still an interesting one in that the current rage of hype being heaped upon our industry has maintained a definite pattern, only now the regulatory hits are not knocking it back down. And this most recent, ever-rising wave is dredging up a mountain of sludge and debris onto our happy little beach that we all have to play in.

In fact, if we were to take a look at the hype cycle today, it might look something like this:

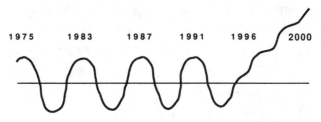

1975          1983          1987          1991          1996          2000

Note, as I mentioned earlier, that each peak is immediately followed by a sharp dip. This is usually due to one or two prominent MLM companies being made examples of by various regulatory agencies, followed by the aforementioned lull (rarely are the attacked companies the most guilty; they're just the most visible). After the big guy gets punished for being too rowdy, everyone calms down and plays nice for a little while. Most take on a very conservative, low hype approach. No one else wants to get caught in the web, plus the actions taken against the target companies usually result in a clear definition of what not to do or say and most try to follow the model.

Unfortunately, like a punished child who promises never to misbehave again, the tendencies gradually return. Everybody's cool, most are playing by the rules, no one is getting in trouble, and the hypsters get lulled into a sense of security. They start taking a few liberties. They start pushing the envelope. They begin to be a little more aggressive in how they present their compensation plan, what people are earning (or how much they *could* earn), and the benefits of their products.

For those of you who were around during the mid-'70s, you may recall prominent MLM programs such as Holiday Magic, Culture Farms, Koscot Interplanetary, and Unimax. All were eventually deemed to be illegal pyramids and closed down. But one company back then fought the "pyramid" label. In fact, that company spent millions of dollars and 4 hard years to defend itself against an attack by not just a state attorney general but the Federal Trade Commission. Fortunately, Amway won that battle and to this day offers a model of what both state and federal authorities look for in a "legal" MLM program—and what you can say about them. What's curious, though, is how well most companies abided by those criteria around 1980 and 1981. I know that 1982 saw a resurgence of at least some amount of hype because I remember being taught how to practice it. Then, in 1983, Herbalife was blasted on both a state and federal level, primarily due to product and income claims, and 1984 through early 1986 was real quiet again. Hardly any hype. Then came United Sciences of America (USA), perhaps the most hyped MLM opportunity in history (and arguably the record holder for first-year growth). While USA was not actually shut down, it was gone by the end of 1987. This was due in part to a barrage of negative press concerning its overzealous promotional campaign. National Safety Associates (NSA) also began to share the burden of antihype scrutiny about that time as well, and 1988 and 1989 were real quite years (relatively speaking, of course, network marketing has never been *completely* void of hype). Then in 1990 things started to heat up. In 1991 practically every windshield in America had a little card on it exclaiming people could earn "$10,000 within 6 to 18 months from today" if they joined NuSkin. Photocopied checks, grossly exaggerated income projections, and curative or anti-aging product claims were pouring through the U.S. Postal Service (again, NuSkin was not nearly the most guilty, just the most visible). Most of us surely recall what the result was—NuSkin was slaughtered in the press and sustained hits from both federal and state regulatory agencies. The next few years the newly reformed NuSkin was the industry model that most companies followed. Photocopied checks, exaggerated income promises, medical claims, and the like were as close to nonexistent during 1992 and 1993 as I've ever remembered it. And sure enough, in 1994 the hype returned. It reached what I thought was surely its peak in 1995. Yet, in 1996 it may have reached record levels not seen since the pre-Amway versus FTC era. I predicted then that if history repeats itself yet again, somebody was about to get killed.

Well, somebody did get killed. A *lot* of somebodies! Boston Finney, Destiny Telecom, Jewelway, and International Heritage were the most prominent of the group (the latter three each claimed well over 100,000 distributors). As of this writing, some wounded but recovering survivors include TravelMax and FutureNet, and Equinox has just been hit with a Temporary Restraining Order (TRO) by the FTC and now has little chance for long-term survival. Although none could claim the prominence of Amway, Herbalife, or NuSkin, surely the combined impact of all of these regulatory attacks, along with many other attacks at the state level on several minor players, would create the same motivation among MLM companies to clean up their acts and not follow the tactics of these target companies. Yet, I see one example after another of companies implementing the very same hype tactics and questionable compensation methods, and they're far *worse* that those who were attacked!

The hype cycle likely has reached such monumental proportions due to the massive proliferation of MLM opportunities entering the market and the resulting increase in competition. To compete in the MLM marketplace today you almost *have* to practice some amount of hype (a sad and perhaps cynical comment, but one that is unfortunately quite true). I've had discussions with various MLM leaders and corporate folk who are, to varying degrees, guilty of hype and I keep hearing the same explanation/excuse: "Our truths are not as good as their lies!" Frankly, although I certainly don't condone the practice of excessive hype, from a strictly business standpoint I can almost see their point. How can a good, honest distributor compete with those who claim their company is signing up "4,000 distributors *per day*," or their comp plan pays "$1,000 with just 25 distributors," or their product "reverses the aging process 20 years." All of these statements are right out of material I've received in just the last few

The hype cycle likely has reached such monumental proportions due to the massive proliferation of MLM opportunities entering the market and the resulting increase in competition.

weeks. Offer after offer claims I'll make tens of thousands of dollars within "a few short weeks." I've got a pile of material here with not only exaggerated income promises and projections (both illegal) but direct claims of income by the distributors themselves—including the resurgence of what was just a few short years ago considered one of the most taboo items one could possibly offer: photocopied checks!

In the past the hype was primarily directed toward compensation plans and income, whereas the trend today is now heavily weighted toward outrageous product claims. Isn't it fascinating how decades-old pharmaceutical companies with access to some of the greatest scientific minds on Earth and billion-dollar research-and-development budgets can't find effective treatments for arthritis, cancer, diabetes, or baldness, but little MLM companies can? Isn't it amazing that someone who discovered a microscopic crystal that makes water freeze at room temperature, improves your car's gas mileage, increases the effectiveness of skin care products by 85%, and cleans your clothes without laundry detergent *isn't* making front-page news all over the world and *isn't* accepting his Nobel Prize, and *is* marketing this miraculous technology through three start-up MLM companies (the first of which was shut down by the state AG, the second failed and was absorbed by the third)? Isn't it just a little curious that a few start-up MLM operations have figured out a way to charge us only $60 per month for "unlimited" long-distance calling and still make a substantial profit, yet AT&T, MCI, and Sprint haven't?

Does anyone else see anything wrong with this picture!?

There also seems to be a glut right now of downline building schemes and fluff programs with grossly overpriced token products. Gimmick marketing is all the rage. Today, everyone claims to have some "revolutionary" new comp plan, product or service, or marketing system. They don't! This is a 53-year-old business, folks. Everything has been tried. Everything you see out there is a variation of stuff that's already been done, over and over. We have half a century of precedent to look back on to know what works and what doesn't work. It's not a secret. We don't have to guess or experiment anymore. And history is telling us—in a loud, booming voice—that traditional, merit-based companies offering legitimate products of value work, and everything else has failed or will fail.

Unfortunately, those traditional, merit-based, network marketing companies offering legitimate products of value have to either try to compete with this bunk or tell people the truth—that success in their program will take time, commitment, patience, hard work, and a financial expense that might even cause them to operate at a loss in the beginning. Of course, if you do, you stand a good chance of being out-hyped by your competition. Hype is designed to recruit you, not inform or educate you. Hype is used to destroy realistic expectations, not create them.

But, there is hope!

I recently ran a series of "anti-hype" display ads in several prominent MLM trade publications. The ads were practically a negative pitch, but they were honest and realistic. I expected the number of responses to drop since the junkies, and those looking for a no-work deal, wouldn't respond, but the quality of the leads we did get would increase. Amazingly, the total response rate has increased by over 50%! I'm becoming more and more convinced that the hypesters are the overzealous, overaggressive minority in this industry. There are still a *lot* of good, professional network marketers out there who understand that, sure, you can keep to the high road and get out-hyped. But, those prospects you lose will inevitably discover the truth sooner or later. And when they do, they are going to remember those that were honest and realistic with them in the past. And, the next time around, *those* people will have all the credibility.

Be the one that they remember.

\* \* \*

MLM companies have been trying for more than a decade to find a quick fix to this stigma surrounding multilevel marketing. Usually they try to change all the words around to make it sound like a different deal. Some will just flat-out deny they are MLM despite the fact that they pay commissions based on multiple levels of distributors, which is the only real criterion. MLM is a commission and marketing system, plain and simple. Either you use this system or you don't. Calling it by a different name, or changing the terms used to define it (or just plain denial of it), doesn't make it not true.

The following article, which was written in early 1999, thoroughly addresses the issue of MLM nomenclature. It also, once again, exemplifies that there are just too darn many MLM companies out there.

At least in this article I had a sense of humor about it.

## The MLM Name Game

AT ONE TIME in the long history of multilevel marketing—decades ago, in fact—there was a great concern by both MLM participants as well as state and federal regulators that there would be an inevitable point of market saturation that would cause the entire industry to come to a painful, grinding halt. Well, in over half a century we've managed to tap less than 10% of the U.S. population (even counting all those who tried it, quit, and will never try it again). Guess that saturation thing isn't going to happen anytime soon.

Well, at least not *distributor* saturation.

Unfortunately, we have another concern. It's *opportunity* saturation.

I read a somewhat amusing article the other day by a well-respected MLM guru who claimed that the network marketing industry is "booming"! His rationale for making this tired, almost cliché exclamation was the massive number of MLM company start-ups that have occurred in recent years and are still occurring today. Now, I don't have a Ph.D. in economics, but I'm pretty sure an industry "booms" when the number of *customers* for a particular product increases on a mass scale, *not* when the number of people *selling* the product increases. This is basic supply and demand. An industry booms when the *demand* booms, not the number of suppliers. In fact, when supply far outstrips demand, it's a strong indicator of a major industry *slump*.

Call me a cynic, call me a pessimist (ah, if I only had a dollar for every time someone did . . . ), but I'd say we've been in an industry-wide slump for about four or five years.

Sure, the number of MLM *companies* is increasing at a phenomenal rate, but many times greater than the demand!

One of many indicators of this "opportunity saturation" is the way companies today are stepping all over each other with their corporate names. I mean, there're only so many ways to combine *life, new, health,* and all or part of *American* before we run out of company names!

I recently did a search of my MLM company database, which contains less than half of the approximately 1,200 companies out there, and found no less than 35 companies with the word *life* in their name. *Thirty-five!* There was *Vision For Life,* and *Nutrition For Life,* and *Renaissance For Life,* and there was just *4Life.* There was *LifeSciences Technologies* and *LifeScience, Inc.,* both of which smushed the first two words together.

There were a mere dozen with the word *health* in the name and seven used the word *body* including *Royal* Body Care, *Total* Body Care, and *Nature's* Body Care (who used to call themselves *Australian* Body Care).

There's Excel, the telecommunications company. But don't stutter when you say their name. People will think you're talking about E-Excel.

The two I get confused by the most are Nato and Natus. And now we also have N.A.T.A.L to go along with Matol.

There's FutureNet, Futurewave, and Future World. And speaking of the future, here's some for you Star Trek fans: Voyager, Trek Alliance, and New Generations. As of this writing, there is no MLM company called Deep Space Nine, Incorporated. Give it time.

I had a contest in my newsletter to see how many MLM companies, living or dead, had the word *way* somewhere in their name. Amazingly, only 10 could be found: Kingsway, Richway, Jewelway, Neways, Greenway, Jetway, Easy Way, MultiWay, American Freeway 100, and of course, Amway. Any others?

The last thing we need is for existing companies to *rename* themselves. Images International claimed, several years ago, that they had to change their name due to a trademark conflict. They became Neways. Recently, Image International launched (now companies are retreading old, abandoned names!). Maybe, to avoid confusion, we could call one company Old Image International and the other one New Image Inter—nope, can't do that. There's *already* a New Image International!

I had a contest in my newsletter to see how many MLM companies, living or dead, had the word *way* somewhere in their name.

Speaking of *new*, apparently there are so few words left that can be attached to the end of this word (NuSkin, New Image, Neways, Nu Directions, Nu Care, Nu Botanical, New Resolution, New Vision . . . ) that a recent start-up decided to just call itself "New." That's it, just *New*. Okay, technically it's New, Inc.

*Image* isn't the only example of resurrecting dead company names either. A few years ago some ex-FundAmerica guys tried to restart that program and called it FundAmerica 2000. Great idea. Let's take a company that was just shut down for being an illegal pyramid scheme, which made the news on every major network in the land, and whose founder was brought up on criminal charges and sent to prison—and call our new company by the same name!

For some reason, no one wanted to join FundAmerica 2000. Strange.

Less than 3 years ago a company ironically titled Momentum went out of business. Personally, and this is just me talking, that's way too soon to be calling a new start-up "Momentum." Even if you put "Health & Nutrition" after it, as one just did.

Why? you might ask.

Because distributors have a penchant for referring to our companies by the fewest possible words, omitting them from right to left. For example, do you really think distributors in "Health Dynamics, a Division of Terra Forma Incorporated" really call themselves that? (Actually, some do—and it's kind of painful to hear them do it.) Let's reduce the words, from right to left, until we get to the minimum that makes sense. Does "Health Dynamics a" make any sense? Mmmm, I think we can go a word or two more. How about just "Health?" Nope, one word too many. And yes, in fact, most reps do call this company "Health Dynamics."

Imagine the confusion between companies like 21st Century Global Network, and 21st Century Nutriceuticals. I recently made a negative remark about the former on my radio show, and got calls and letters from the latter who were not at all happy. Why? Because I did the same thing! I lopped off "Global Network," as most others do, and just called them "21st Century." You'd think this problem was solved when 21st Century Global Network was absorbed by Legacy USA. But, alas, we still have 21st Century Collectables and 21st Century Network! What's more, Legacy Health Solutions will likely use the same minimalist method that Legacy USA reps will use—and they're both call themselves "Legacy."

Fortunately, Legacy Lifeline is no longer with us. Well, at least until some new start-up thinks it's a cool name.

Not all companies with similar names will suffer much confusion in the market. For example, Heritage Health Products, which is commonly referred to by their own reps as just "Heritage," won't have to worry about folks getting them confused with the now defunct International Heritage Inc. You can drop the "Inc." but that's about it. IHI was rarely referred to as just "Heritage" because that would require dropping a word from the front end. Never happens.

Another example would be Longevity Network (drop the Network, call it Longevity), and American Longevity (can't drop a word from the front, so it's always the whole "American Longevity"). Weird hybrid names like Youngevity (yes, there really is one) shouldn't be any challenge either.

Okay, so what about Mannatech? (By the way, it used to be called Emprise. When there's a shortage, corporate names should be rationed one to a company!) You'd sure think this company name would remain unique, wouldn't you? Well, ask a MannaValley distributor. Of course, when the words are conjoined you don't drop one. I don't think anyone's going to claim to be a distributor for "Manna."

Rumor has it that the management of Renaissance For Life was fit to be tied when some folks who spun off of Destiny (Telecom) started another calling card deal and called it Renaissance USA. And, you bet, everybody was calling them both just "Renaissance."

Because there is at least a 95% failure rate among start-up MLMs, most of these name overlaps take care of themselves, as was the case with the extra Renaissance. But, here's the ironic twist to this story. The owner of Renaissance For Life launched yet another MLM company (calling it a sub-division) and named it Advantage International Marketing. There's no other company with a first name of "Advantage" (is there?), so what's the problem?

Well, there's one more thing we all love to do with our company names—make acronyms out of them. Right? Nutrition For Life is NFL. American Communications Network is ACN. National Safety Associates is NSA. Staff Of Life *was* SOL (which probably explains why they changed their name to R-Garden). So, guess what Advantage International Marketing is called? That's right. AIM. Guess what the much older American Image Marketing is called? That's right. AIM!

Some companies have really cool names. I like Usana (anything with the word *sauna* in the title works for me). Longevity. Integris. Achievers. I like the name Vaxä, even though I have no idea what it means. And I've always liked the old, homey sound of Watkins. Thank God the founder wasn't named Manson, huh?

In their apparent desperation to come up with a neat company name, with so few still remaining, some companies, it seems, had to take from the bottom of the barrel.

I've never liked the name "Changes." I know how much we distributors hate changes—that is, perpetual changes to the comp plan, changes to the products, changes to the marketing system, *changes* to the *company name* . . . I don't want changes, I want consistency. I want solidity. I want to be a distributor for *Stability International!*

Or, how about Jackpot International? Or, Millionaire Maker's Inc.? Or, Easy Street International? Why not just get a megahorn and stand outside your state Attorney General's office and yell, "We're a pyramid scheme, we're a money game, investigate us please!" (I'm not saying they are, but why create a name that makes it *sound* like you are?)

And who came up with the idea to launch a company called Y2K International? Why not call it Paranoia International, or Hysteria International, or how about Armageddon International?

I wonder, what is Y2K International going to call itself *next year?* Y2K1?

No discussion of the MLM name game would be complete unless we gave a little attention to the screwy games we play with what we call this entire industry.

Back in the 1950s, when Shaklee and Amway first began, this form of business was called only one thing— multilevel marketing. Today, you may hear it referred to as Personal Marketing, Consumer Direct Marketing, Direct to Market Selling, Direct Marketing, Home Marketing, Dual Marketing, and unfortunately, even Pyramid Sales (with no negative connotation intended). I've even heard it referred to as Multiple Layer Retailing, and The UnFranchise. Give me a break!

The most common alternative title is, of course, *network* marketing.

Why so many aliases? I theorize that it has a lot to do with the negative image that the term multilevel marketing still brings with it. So many people still associate this term with pyramid schemes, fly-by-night rip-offs, home party demonstrations, door-to-door sales, and really boring products like soap and scrub brushes. One way to avoid this stigma is to create a whole new identity. I think companies just wanted to present a new, fresh image of the business.

I once called a Mary Kay representative, many years ago before I knew better, and told her I was interested in getting information on multilevel marketing businesses. She curtly told me that Mary Kay is *not* a multilevel marketing company. They use a form of business called "Dual" marketing. When I questioned further as to the nature of this seemingly new way of doing business, she explained that in dual marketing you make money two ways. You can buy the products wholesale from the company and resell at a profit, or you can sponsor others to sell them and you make a commission. Duel. Two ways. I was still confused.

When I asked her if these people you sponsor can also sponsor others into the business, and do you receive a commission off their sales as well, she said definitely yes. Okay. So all these people are marketing the products? Yes, she replied. And they are marketing the products on different levels below you? Yes. On multiple levels? Yes. They're marketing the products on multiple levels? Yes. So it's multilevel marketing? NO! It's *dual* marketing.

I really question whether all these pseudonyms have much effect on uninformed prospects, anyway. Many times

I've used the term network marketing, only to have my prospect respond with, "Oh, that's like multilevel marketing, isn't it?" When I agree, they sometimes come back with, "Is this like one of those pyramid schemes?" Very rarely do they not do the math.

Call it what you will, it's all multilevel marketing in the literal sense. They're all marketing products on multiple levels.

If anything, I think we should just all just stick with MLM or network marketing. Anything else might seem as if we'll trying to hide something—as if we're not too proud of what we're *really* offering.

If that's how you really feel, best you call it quits.

## Discussion

I think it's unfortunate that Mary Kay has taken such a hard line against acknowledging its MLM roots. I look at all these other MLM distributors out there crying and moaning about how "unfair" their programs are, and most are a cakewalk compared to what's required of Mary Kay reps. Yet, these women not only don't make a big stink about their plan being too hard, they actually succeed with it. They know exactly what they're getting into from the beginning, and most tend to treat the opportunity as a serious business. They're very professional. I just wish they'd lose the term Dual Marketing and join the club. We need them.

I had a semi-regular column in *MarketWave* called "In The Dog House." Usually it's a facetious little column directed more toward individuals who are in hot water with us, rather than companies, and it's usually not taken too seriously—by our readers or me.

In one recent column, though, I really took to task a well-known MLM company (specifically their president and CEO) for claiming not only that this was not a multilevel marketing opportunity, but the reason it wasn't was because MLM opportunities involve big hype, front-loading of products, singing and chanting, products of little value, and only recruitment-focused "get rich quick" promotions. The CEO even suggested, rather ironically, that MLMs typically hide the true nature of their business.

Now we've got MLM company presidents bashing MLM. Is this a bad dream?

The semantic game-playing that's going on with these companies sometimes goes beyond just changing the name of their form of marketing. Some have changed the names of many of the terms they use in their business. For example, Mary Kay doesn't have break-away groups, they are "offspring" groups. It doesn't have levels, it has "tiers." So, I guess if I call the cab of my Mitsubishi a "cockpit," my tires "landing gear," the louvers "ailerons," and the body a "fuselage," then I could rightfully claim to be an airline pilot!

Companies like these can call themselves whatever they want, and perhaps they'll fool a few naive distributors. But the majority of those in this industry, as well as state and federal regulatory agencies, won't buy it for a minute. Like it or not, these pseudo-named MLM companies will be forever bound to MLM by an unseverable chain. If this ship we call multilevel marketing ever sinks, they're going to the bottom right along with it. And we do seem to be taking on a little water.

I would strongly suggest to these companies that rather than trying to saw through the chain, they might want to grab a bucket.

*   *   *

Many network marketers today have made a science out of imparting illusionary or deceptive information with

**If** I call the cab of my Mitsubishi a "cockpit," my tires "landing gear," the louvers "ailerons," and the body a "fuselage," then I could rightfully claim to be an airline pilot!

technically truthful statements. The following article is a conglomerate of some of the very best examples. These are also great examples of claims you may have to defend against.

## Romantic Semantics: Deciphering MLM's Secret Language

*Romantic:* Imaginative, but impractical; not based on fact, imaginary.

*Semantics:* The study of meaning in language form with regard to its historical change.

These definitions courtesy of the *American Heritage Dictionary*. So, how does this apply to network marketing? Let us count the ways.

Network marketers have, over the last half century, evolved into some of the greatest spin doctors and wordsmiths that our society has ever created. We've become masters at romancing our semantics. That is, we as an industry

have created this wonderful, albeit misleading and illusionary, way of stating facts. As paradoxical as that may sound
(illusionary facts?), practically every line of every ad, and
every sentence spoken at a typical opportunity meeting,
now contain some degree of evidence of this. To wit . . .

"No, we don't accept credit cards . . . we're in the business of getting people out of debt, not further in debt!"

I didn't make that one up. A prominent MLM company made this exclamation several years ago—after burn-
ing through 22 Merchant Service providers that refused to
accept their account—the proverbial lemonade out of
lemons.

How about this classic: "We are absolutely debt-free!"
Translation: "No one will lend us money!" Now, understand. I'm sure there are many MLM companies who are
debt-free because they pay for everything with cash, and
they can comfortably afford to do so. Good for them. But,
how do you know? Simply proclaiming yourself debt-free
certainly *implies* you're cash rich and financially prudent, or
it could mean you can't initiate credit terms, or you've
screwed so many of your vendors in the past they'll only do
business with you on a cash basis. The latter scenario would
likely signal the death knell of the company. Yet, they could
still claim, "We are absolutely debt-free!" and they would be
absolutely telling the truth. Another paradox. Dishonest
honesty.

Another way a company can claim to be debt-free is by
simply not counting all the things they owe money for. For
example, isn't "accrued commission owed" a debt? Actually,
I'd like my company to have a *lot* of that debt each month.

What about payroll or sales taxes that are collected and paid quarterly? Technically, these are all forms of debt. So, just ignore them and then you're debt-free!

Several years ago, this same logic was used by the second baseman on my Little League team. After losing the final game of the season by a goodly margin, and all but 3 of the previous 17 games, this curly-haired little 7-year-old attempted to comfort me by exclaiming, "Ya' know, coach, not counting all the games we lost, we were *under-feated!*"

This also reminds me of the debate regarding whether legalizing drugs would affect the crime rate. Advocates of this idea claim the crime rate would drop dramatically. Of course it would! If you make fewer things illegal, fewer laws will be broken. Hey, why don't we just declare everything legal? Then we would have virtually no crime!

I've always loved this one: "We're approaching momentum!" Now, if we were to make the logical assumption that all MLM companies will eventually achieve some degree of fast growth if they stay in business long enough, practically *any* company could make this claim. But, what exactly *is* momentum? Is it 50% growth in one month, or 100% monthly growth over 3 months, or 1,000% in a week? Well, let's take a look at one recent situation. An MLM company that was more than 10 years old had never received more than 350 applications in a single day. That was their record. Then, one recent Thursday, out of nowhere, 800 apps swamped the home office. The next day, 1,300 more! Some of their distributors rode through MLMville yelling "Momentum is coming! Momentum is coming!" Was it? Sounds like it, doesn't it? But, let's take a peek behind the scenes. This company had a $295 enrollment package (I've changed the details here just slightly to protect the innocent). They had also just absorbed the distributor base of another MLM company. This new influx of distributors were given a grace period to re-enroll and have the $295 fee waived. Guess when the deadline was? That's right. Five o'clock that Friday.

Pay no attention to that man behind the curtain.

Let's stay with this issue of "momentum" a bit longer. This is surely one of the most romanticized words in the MLM vocabulary. What exactly is "approaching?" A common MLM myth that continues to go in and out of remission is that MLM companies hit momentum when they reach $50 million in annual sales. The truth is, one company out of thousands, over the last 53 years, went into momentum at that point (NuSkin around 1990). Not one before, not one since. But, for some reason, that's now the accepted benchmark by many MLM romantics. So, when they boldly claim that their company is going into momentum soon because they are "approaching $50 million in annual sales," are they being truthful? It's hard not to be. If that company had sales last month of $10, and sales this month were $20, they are, in fact, "approaching" $50 million in annual sales.

*Rationalizing:* Lying with a clear conscience.

That's the *Clements Dictionary* definition.

Here're a few other recent examples. I'll just run through them quickly.

"We're listed with the Better Business Bureau!" One of the most common ways a company gets "listed" with the

BBB is by having complaints registered against it. A company *chooses* to be a *member*.

"(Fill in the blank) has been nominated for a Nobel Prize!" I can nominate my cat for a Nobel Prize.

"(Fill in the blank) has previously owned/operated two multi-million-dollar network marketing companies!" Mohammed Ali wanted to be "four-time heavyweight champion." To achieve this feat required that he *lose* at least three times. So, if so-and-so *used* to own and operate other MLM companies, what happened to them? They went out of business? They were shut down? The shareholders booted him out? He sold his interest and is now starting another MLM company in competition with his old company? The possibilities are myriad. None of them are good.

"Our products are listed in the *Physician's Desk Reference*." The PDR lists what you pay them to. The publisher "does not warrant or guarantee," nor has it performed "any independent analysis," nor is it "advocating the use of" any product found therein. That's straight from the forward of the 47th edition.

"Our product is a $60 billion industry!" In other words, you're trying to sell something everyone already possesses?

"We don't sell lotions and potions!" So, you've intentionally avoided the one product niche that the largest, most successful MLM companies and richest distributors are all involved in? That's a selling point?

"No meetings!" So, you don't offer what has been proven to be the single most effective enrollment and training method throughout MLM history? This is a benefit?

"No selling!" So, you're . . . lying?

"Our infinity bonus pays 10% down to the first Executive Director in the leg." Translation: "Our infinity bonus pays down a few more levels and then stops."

Mr. Webster and I have a very different definition of *infinity* than many MLM companies. I'm pretty sure infinity means "*doesn't stop.*"

*Sarcasm:* A mocking or contemptuously ironic remark.

Here are more illusionary benefits . . .

"We allow you to enroll your spouse (or yourself) on your own first level!" An illusionary benefit based on the illusion you're the only one who benefits. If *everyone else* has the same benefit, and they're all double-dipping too, then sure, you get paid double—on half the volume!

"No (or little tiny) monthly personal volume requirement!" So, you create this big downline full of people all sitting around waiting for someone else to order something. If you don't have to order very much, then *they* don't have to order very much.

"You can earn overrides on your own personal volume!" This essentially amounts to a rebate. Problem is, it's really just a tax-free loan to the company that you will pay income tax on *twice!* Think about it. You pay $10 of already taxed income for a bottle of vitamins. The company keeps it for a month, then pays you back $2 *of your own money.* They got free use of your money for a month, Uncle Sam says that $2 is new income, and you get double taxed—instead of just charging you $8 for the vitamins. The company benefits in two ways: financially, and by creating good will. The distributors actually think the company is doing them a favor!

Here's my all time favorite: "We sell our service at slightly below cost, but we make it up in volume." I think we should pause for a moment on that one.

Okay, let's continue.

"(Fill in the company) was 10 years in development!" So, the founder *thought* about it for nine years, and spent the last year putting everything together?

"We're in prelaunch!" The birth of an MLM company is no different than the birth of a baby. You're never in "pre-birth." Either you're born, or your not. Either your processing applications, shipping product, and cutting checks, or you're not. "Prelaunch" is nothing more than a marketing gimmick to entice the naive newcomer to MLM who still believes there is an inherent advantage to "getting in at the top." Some companies have romanced this illusion for literally years! I know one company that claimed they were in prelaunch in their *third year of business!*

**H**ere's my all time favorite: "We sell our service at slightly below cost, but we make it up in volume." I think we should pause for a moment on that one.

"Ground floor" is abused in much the same manner. Some companies are now defining ground floor by the relatively small number of distributors they have, not their age. One such company recently claimed to be a ground-floor opportunity even though it was over 10 years old!

Statistics can be romanced as well. And when you couch them in well played semantics, the results can go from ridiculous to dangerous.

"You can earn up to $60,000 per month, or more!" Read this very real ad headline carefully. It essentially covers every number from zero to infinity. The ultimate "truth in advertising."

"Over 300,000 people have joined our company!" This was also a true statement at the time. Of course, the ad forgot to mention that 230,000 had since quit. Note, it doesn't say they *have* 300,000, it says that's how many "have joined."

Along those same lines, several less-than-5-year-old MLM companies today are bragging about their distributor base of over 500,000. The catch is, they are counting how many sequential ID numbers they have given out throughout their history. Each could lose 50,000 reps next month, and gain 1,000 new ones, and that number will go *up* to 501,000.

Dictionary definition of *hype:* To increase artificially.

And speaking of less-than-5-year-old companies, have you heard this one? "Only 26 (29?, 32?, 36?) MLM companies have made it to their fifth anniversary." The most ironic thing about this wholly incorrect claim (I have 79 such companies in my database) is that it was popularized by a leading distributor for a company that had not yet celebrated its fifth anniversary. The intent here, obviously, was to scare prospects away from less-than-5-year-old companies. The reality is that the vast majority of MLM failures occur within the first 2 years. So, to then suggest that the vast majority fail within the first 5 years would be an accurate statement, would it not? But then, so would "The vast majority of MLM companies fail within the first 20 years."

Of course, you'd only say that if you were involved in a 21-year-old company.

But the illogic of this scare-tactic propaganda goes even deeper. Even if the previously-mentioned 26-company figure were accurate, it still wouldn't really mean what it's intended to mean. Of all the MLM companies that have ever existed in the last 53 years, the vast majority launched this decade! Of course there are very few old MLM companies. Using the same illogic I can prove that my Ford Model T is better built and lasted longer than a Lexus. After all, of all the cars still on the road after 75 years of use, almost all are Model T's and not one is a Lexus.

This one drives me nuts: "If you get four people who each get four, you can make $800 with just 20 people!" These types of pitches will even be referred to as "conservative." They are also assuming that every single distributor that you enroll will enroll four others, and that the bottom 16 will never quit even though they have no downline themselves, in fact *no one* ever quits, and *every single distributor* in your downline *always* orders each month.

*Conservative:* Moderate; cautious; restrained; erring toward the negative.

And what about those really low attrition rates we keep hearing about? Is a 6% attrition rate good? Sounds pretty good—if they're talking about last year, or over the life of the company. Or, are they referring to yesterday? Or last week? We don't know. They never say. Wonder why.

Reorder rates can be manipulated in much the same way. More than one popular program has recently claimed a "75% monthly reorder rate." Okay, so 100 people order in January. Seventy five reorder in February. Then, 75% of them, or 56 people, reorder in March, and 42 in April, 32 in May, 24 in June . . . I think you see where this is going. Twelve months later you'll have no customers left—and still be able to honestly claim a 75% monthly reorder rate. Technically.

A few years ago a company claimed that 93% of all those surveyed had lost weight on their diet products. What wasn't revealed was that only those who had been on the product for at least six months were part of the survey. What a concept. Let's find out how many people got results from our product by only surveying those people who got results from our product. What I can't figure out is why the other 7% kept ordering!

"There are lies, damn lies, and statistics." —Mark Twain

The aloe wars of the early '90s saw their share of data 'romancing. One company said right on their 16-ounce bottle, "This bottle contains 100% pure Aloe Vera." A competitor had the product assayed. It contained 1 ounce of pure Aloe Vera, and 15 ounces of water and flavoring. They sued, claiming false advertising. They lost. The bottle did indeed "contain 100% pure Aloe Vera," as well as water and flavoring.

Sales figures have seen more romance than a Harlequin novel. One popular company claimed sales in the hundreds of millions. Upon closer review, I found that almost half of their "sales" were the training packages they were charging their distributors, not the product they were in the business of selling. In fact, "sales" included administrative fees, shipping charges, marketing tools, and other such items. I guess a sale is a sale. Another company recently claimed a monthly sales figure of $8.5 million. Of course, they were quoting "retail" sales . . . and they have a 100% suggested markup . . . and an 8-ounce bottle of shampoo wholesaled for $12.50 ($25 suggested retail). They have free distributor enrollment, so their products are probably never *retailed*, ever . . . so their *actual* sales were exactly *half* the number they were promoting.

There's an old saying, "If you torture the data long enough you can make it say anything." It seems you can romance it into doing your bidding as well.

Do we, as an industry, tend to romance our incomes, just a little? Like, when people say, "My income has reached $50,000 per month!" Notice they didn't actually tell you they were making 50 grand right now; they clearly said their income "has reached" that level. That was in back in 1989. They're only making $5,000 now and have $6,000 in monthly expenses. Unfortunately, I'm only exaggerating just a little.

I actually find it quite amusing when I hear these hucksters claim they were making some huge income in another MLM program, and they just "walked away" from it to join this hot, earth-shaking, revolutionary new start-up deal. Obviously, there's always more to the story. Like, they *sold* their old downline, or their distributorship was terminated, or the company just filed Chapter 7. It's easy to walk away from a $50,000 check—when it bounces. One "heavy hitter" called me recently to proclaim he'd just walked away from a *one . . . hundred . . . thousand . . .* dollar monthly income. True story. Even if his story were all true, you know why I'd never want to be enrolled by this guy? Because I wouldn't want an idiot for a sponsor! Or, someone who thought I was.

Folks, when my income gets to $100,000 per month, I'm going to brand my company's logo onto my forehead!

Please understand, I'm not suggesting that every positive claim or impressive statistic about network marketing is bogus. In fact, as cynical as I've become about this business, I still believe the "pros" (professionals) outnumber the "cons" (convicts). The desperate, aggressive, overzealous *minority* of MLMers out there just seem to be the ones who are always in our face. They stand out.

Network marketing is good. Very good. There's no shortage of positive information out there. I'm just balancing the scale. This is the secret behind the trick. Take away the smoke and mirrors and the illusion loses its ability to persuade.

Romance the truth. It's okay. Hype is powerless against it.

## Discussion

A couple other "benefits" are commonly cited by distributors that don't really involve romancing semantics, per se, but are worthy of a brief discussion.

First, there's the selling point, "We manufacture our own products." This is usually presented as a great advantage since there's one less middle-man, thus lower priced products and/or more margin to contribute to the comp plan. However, most (but certainly not all) MLM companies that hype this "advantage" are not the actual manufacturer of the products at all. They are manufactured at another location by another company that might be wholly owned and controlled by the MLM company, but it's still a company that needs to pay its bills and make a profit. Therefore, the products are going through the same chain of distribution as any other MLM company. This probably explains why, for the most part, the companies today that claim to produce their own products don't offer any significant price or comp plan advantage.

A better question might be, Who *designed* the products, and why? In other words, was there some actual science behind it, or were the products just cranked out so everyone would have an excuse to exchange cash? Many MLM operations today were launched by ex-distributors who got the idea to start an MLM company first, then asked "Now, what can we sell?" Then they went to a private labeler and had some vitamins and shampoo produced the cheapest possible way so as to create the most margin so they could afford "the highest pay out in the industry." However, a number of good MLM companies today were born out of a desire to move an already existing product to the masses in the most effective manner, thus the decision to market them via network marketing. In other words, the product came first, not the opportunity.

Next, there's the issue of being a public company. Is this an advantage? Well, depends. Certainly it would suggest the company has greater financially stability, or at least that's what most prospects seem to assume. Also, when times are good, and the company is growing and profitable, you can make such claims with far more credibility simply because there's evidence to back you up. However, when things are not so good and profits begin to drop, you have to publicly reveal your losses, which is not the case with a privately held company. MLM distributors tend to spook easily, and a couple of bad quarters in a row could create a severe lack of confidence in the field, and greater attrition—thus creating yet another bad quarter.

Going public is great when everything's beautiful, but when it turns ugly, you can't wear makeup.

* * *

Many of my past occupations have involved close contact, at least on a psychological level, with a large number of people. My very first real job was a cook at Taco Bell. The food production phase of my career wasn't very challenging because everything Taco Bell offered then was essentially beans, ground beef, lettuce, and cheese just folded different ways (lay it flat, you had a tostada; fold it once, you had a taco; roll it up, you had a burrito). My "promotion" to the front counter provided my first glimpse into the workings of the average American mind on a mass scale. And it was scary.

> **G**oing public is great when everything's beautiful, but when it turns ugly, you can't wear makeup.

I also spent 16 years as a professional umpire (Little League to semi-pro). I learned far more about the nature of human reasoning (or lack of such) from the people in the stands than I did from the players or coaches. And it was even scarier.

Then I opened my own computer time rental and training business—right on the border of San Francisco's Mission and Castro districts. I'm not going to elaborate, other than to say it was the most disturbing 6 years of my life. I did more than leave my heart in San Francisco; I left my car, my clothes, my furniture—I couldn't get out of there fast enough!

(A personal note to all Bay Area readers: Yes, I do believe San Francisco is a beautiful city—from high up, far away, at night.)

Enter network marketing. Despite my past endeavors to understand the human condition, nothing prepared me for this. Network marketers have their own, unique eccentricities. Their own original style of reasoning. And after 17 years of working with uplines, downlines, and crosslines, I've started to wonder . . .

## Does MLM Make Us Goofy?

MY 10 YEARS as one of the MLM industry watchdogs has involved several hundred hours of reading various MLM-related books, newsletters, and magazines and having conversations with literally thousands of MLM participants, vendors, trainers, and owners. Over this period, I have concluded that something about the MLM industry is making quite a few of us really goofy. Perhaps our "herbal formulas" contain more herbs than we know about. Or, maybe it's the radiation we've absorbed from watching all those videos. It could be that pressing a phone against your head 6 to 8 hours a day cuts off blood vessels to your brain. All I know is, something is going on here.

A classic example is a conversation I had about 6 years ago with a local print-shop owner. A print shop, by the way, that claimed to have several MLM clients.

I called this printer to get a quote on reprinting a limited number of back issues of *MarketWave*. She said they had a special deal where all double-sided, 11 × 17 pages would be 15¢ per sheet. I then asked (remember, this is the owner I'm talking to) what would be the fewest number they could print. She replied that they could print whatever amount I needed. Okay, what about 10? Well, she said, they really couldn't print that few. She then explained to me about setup costs, labor, and various other fixed costs. Fair enough. So exactly what is the least number you could print, I asked. She again replied, "As I said sir, we can print any amount you wish."

Uh oh.

"How about 20?" I ventured. Nope. Couldn't print that few either. It just wouldn't be cost-effective, you see, because of those fixed costs, which she began to list again.

Now, I had already tried *fewest* and *least*. I wouldn't dare try *minimum*. That's another whole syllable. Ah, what the heck, I thought, let's give it a try.

"All right. So exactly what is the *minimum* number of sheets that you can print?"

"Sir," she responded, obviously getting annoyed, "like I said, we can print whatever number you like, we just can't print that few."

Believe it or not, we went through this loop about three more times, each time with me raising the requested number by 10, followed by her desperately trying to get through my thick skull that they could print whatever amount I needed—except for every amount I requested.

The call ended with me (whom my Little League team used to call "Spock" because of my inability to get riled) yelling into the phone "51, 52, 53, 54, . . . Stop me when I hit a number you can print!"

She hung up on me.

To this day, I still don't know the least, fewest, minimum number of pages she could print for me. And I never will. She went out of business—just like the MLM company she was a distributor for (Consumer's Buyline).

The logic portion of the brain seems to be most affected by MLM exposure. More evidence of this can be found in the ads we place. Just recently I saw one with the headline "Little Known Secrets . . ." What other kind of secrets are there? Well-known secrets?

Or, how about this one: "Brand New MLM Now Launching!" Have you ever seen an old MLM company launch?

Or, how about this logic buster: "Earn income through the retail sale of our free reports!"

Here's another headline I just saw that you can add to your list: "The MLM Learing Group." I mean, how does this happen? Learing? I liken these types of mega-typos to a pedestrian being accidentally hit by a train in broad daylight. I occasionally hear about this happening, and as morbid as it is, I almost want to be there to see exactly how such an event could occur. When a typesetter keys in a headline such as "Credit Problems, Money Troubles, Down On Your

Lick?" (actual copy), does he not look up and read what he just typed at least once?

Here are a few more true stories from the annals of *MarketWave.*

I got a call about 2 months ago from a distraught man who was incensed that I did not have a system in place to provide him with a sample copy of my newsletter. He and his wife were roaming the country in his motor home, you see. And yes, he was quite serious.

Another man called recently to order a subscription and a back issue. When I explained that there was a $2 shipping and handling charge on the back issue, he protested that since I had to send the first issue of his subscription anyway, why was he being charged for the shipping on the back issue? (An argument that has come up more than once, by the way.) I explained that there was additional postage, and back issues were all hand-folded and collated and were more expensive to produce because they are reprinted in limited quantity. He wasn't buying it. Literally. He bluntly stated that he would cancel his order if the $2 was charged. I later discovered that this guy earns in excess of $13,000 per month in a well-known MLM program. That's 13 thousand dollars—two of which he got to keep that day.

Just recently a new MLMer, who sounded way too young to have already been so affected, called my voice mail and requested a sample copy of my newsletter. His message was as follows: "Yes, this is John Smith from Tampa, Florida, and I just read your article in *Network Marketing Today* magazine. I would like to get the sample copy as soon as possible and I will send you the dollar you requested. Thank you." Click.

The real frustrating part is that Mr. Smith (not his real name) is the third person to leave such a message so far this year! And that's not counting the two by Mr. Smith himself, who's still wondering where his sample copy is and whose address I still don't know.

I can't count the number of times, especially in the early years of *MarketWave*, that I would fax information requests or a series of questions regarding the company I was reviewing, only to have every one completely ignored. Or I made numerous calls to the corporate office to talk to the president or VP regarding questions or concerns that I didn't feel comfortable asking distributors, and never had a single call returned. And then, after the review is published, I get a call or letter from the president chastising me for not getting my facts straight.

Actually, that's not a good example of being goofy, that's just me venting. Thanks for indulging me.

Goofy? How about the infamous MetChem scandal? This was a bogus review I did (as an April Fool's joke) for a scheme where you could get paid $6 for every tin can you sent in (because MetChem found a way to convert tin into platinum, you see). Honestly, it's not the fact that 16 of my subscribers called to get the address for MetChem (after all, the information was supposed to be coming from a reputable source—me!). It's the fact that the instructions to order the information clearly stated "Go sit in the corner. Haven't we taught you anything?" then asked that you spell out the first letters of each sentence of the first paragraph—which spelled

April fools. Fortunately, 12 of them called back to ask that I ignore their previous request. Good for them. The others (and you know who you are) claimed they followed the instructions perfectly—and still wanted the address!

Perhaps the silliest *actual* product I've ever seen offered by an MLM company (and there's a lot of competition for this honor) was one called "Vitamin O." The company claimed that many illnesses today are caused by lack of oxygen in the bloodstream. By popping these rather expensive oxygen capsules, you'd supplement your body's oxygen supply by absorbing it through the lining of the small intestines. Besides the fact that any high school student who got a B- in Science & Anatomy would know that oxygen isn't absorbed by the intestines (I think there's another organ designed to do that, called *lungs*), just plain common sense would suggest that we could achieve the same benefit by just hyperventilating for 30 seconds, a couple times a day—for free!

So far, I've received four death threats. Three were just a prank (I'm pretty sure), but the other seemed quite serious. This angry, anonymous caller was upset that I had "trashed" his opportunity and that my review was "sinful." That review resulted in the third highest rated opportunity ever featured in *MarketWave*, and the highest for the year in which the call was made. Wadda' they want from me already!

While we're on the cheery subject of death threats, one of the funniest ones was from a guy who, during a long, rambling message, attacked the content of a classified ad I had just run in *USA Today*, and then told me about how he was going to come by my house and "blow your head off with my AK-47." That wasn't the funny part. He also included a specific time and date (Saturday at three o'clock) and made the call to my company 800 number! In case you're not familiar with how most 800 numbers work, you get a list of all incoming phone numbers with your bill, and some services, like the one I work with, give you the ability to hit a number on your telephone key pad and it reads back the phone number of the caller immediately. What's even funnier is that the caller's phone number was the exact same phone number of the previous caller—who left his entire name, address, and phone number in response to our advertised offer!

Last month I had a discussion with a man who was dissatisfied with the performance of his current company's compensation plan (we'll call his company Generic International). He called to ask me about the plan I was working. I told him the type, and he replied, "Eh, I was hoping to stay with a plan like Generic's." I then explained the payout. "Hmmm. Actually, I kind of like an even payout—like Generic's." I forged on. After explaining the qualifications, he responded by explaining to me why he liked the way "Generic was doing it." The conversation eventually went beyond comp plans to products. After telling him about mine, sure enough, he was hoping to stay with products "like Generic has." He stayed with Generic International.

I recently came across a distributor-produced full-page ad for an MLM opportunity within which the distributor described his company's great new support tool—an automated downline and sales volume tracking system. Nothing wrong with that, except that when describing how simple the steps were to use the system he used his *actual* ID number and password! Yes, of course I called and accessed the system (I'm not nosy, I'm inquisitive). This guy, who was claiming to have achieved great success with this opportunity, had 115 people on his first level alone, but his total commission earned for the past month was $26! The headline of his ad read: "My 10 years of MLM frustration." I have a theory about that.

Another MLM company I was preparing to review sent an open letter to all of its distributors chastising them for accepting returns of their weight-loss product. It seems many of them were returning the 30-day supply of product with only a few of the capsules consumed. The author of this letter, their national marketing director, claimed that customers must use all 30 days' worth of product to get any results. Therefore, in spite of their "100% money-back guarantee" on retail customer returns, the company would no longer provide refunds on unfinished product returned by its distributors—unless the bottle was returned empty! Hmmm. There's got to be a way around this policy. Let's think hard.

A discussion of goofiness in network marketing cannot end without at least a mention of those folks who claim to have depleted their life savings to purchase huge inventory loads upon joining an MLM opportunity (the highest I've heard of is $120,000). Or those who leave high-paying, secure jobs to work an MLM opportunity full time after only a few weeks or months of success. I just read about a

Long Island man who left a $192,000-a-year job to work at FundAmerica back in early 1990. Bad timing. Bad.

NGS (Networking Goofiness Syndrome) seems to be spreading in epidemic proportions. This dreaded malady must be stopped before the end of the 1990s, when, allegedly according to *The Wall Street Journal*, 65% of all goods and services will be moved by way of network marketing. Unknowing college and university professors all over the country are now teaching people how to inflict themselves with NGS. Even Donald Trump claimed he would risk exposure to NGS by pursuing network marketing should he ever lose his fortune again. (All of the preceding statements are ridiculous, yet common, MLM myths. They are completely untrue. Don't repeat them, please.)

Fortunately, despite all of the massive exposure I've had to network marketing over a prolonged period of time, I personally seem to have been completely unaffected. I have experienced no symptoms of NGS of any kind.

By the way, not to change the subject, but I want all of my readers to be aware that I no longer wish to be referred to by my given name, but rather by this unpronounceable symbol:

Thank you for your cooperation.

## Discussion

Since I wrote this article, I've spent 2 months working out of the home office of an MLM company. I could probably produce a three-volume set of books on NGS from just that experience. Have you ever seen an entire product order written small enough to fit in the memo section of a check? I have. One letter to the president of the company (to the *president*) was more cute than goofy. It was from a nice lady who was having trouble getting her product delivered, so she included detailed information on how to find her house (go down the dirt road for 2 miles, turn left at the big willow tree . . . ).

I also got to handle a complaint to the attorney general of Washington (remember, the one who laughed?) that involved a lady who completely filled out and signed a form to apply for a monthly Electronic Funds Transfer (EFT) of $25 (a standard feature in many MLM programs). She even included the requisite voided check. When $25 was automatically deducted from her account the following month, she fired off a scathing letter to the Washington Consumer Fraud Division. She claimed this company had actually "removed" funds from her account "without my signature." She even included a copy of the EFT paper draft! She demanded that these dishonest crooks be shut down immediately! They sent her $25 back.

I now have a whole new perspective on the inner workings of MLM companies. I've also gained an abundance of respect and empathy for MLM corporate people. I wouldn't have their jobs for a million dollars. A million-five maybe, but not a million.

For those of you who have trouble recognizing sarcasm (even when it's so thick it drips off the page into your lap), I don't really think MLM makes people goofy. I think most of us are pretty goofy already. Case in point: The Coca-Cola Company claims it has received hundreds of letters all wanting to know the same thing—are those Coke-drinking, ice-skating, belly-luging, star-gazing polar bears in their TV commercials real? True story.

Just imagine what would happen if Coca-Cola ever went MLM!

# CHAPTER TWO

# What We Should Be Doing (But Are Not)

B Y "WE" I am referring to the entire MLM industry. Obviously many of you *are* using many of the techniques and ideas found in this chapter. Unfortunately, most of us are not.

While MLM goofiness is still fresh in our minds, let's begin with the aforementioned list of my favorite MLM and mail-order ad headlines. Keep in mind, these are not made up. Every one is an actual headline. I only emphasize that because it's going to be really hard to believe.

## MLM and Mail-Order Advertising at Its Weirdest: My All-Time Top Favorites!

FOR YEARS I'VE read the various MLM trade publications, card decks, and mail-order solicitations, and I have often laughed, and sometimes cringed, at some of the bogus

95

claims, typos, and not-so-professional ad copy. I have collected these ads in a separate file for about the last 10 months. Some I remember from years past. This is a collection of my personal favorites.

To protect the innocent, the advertisers themselves, the publication or card deck in which the ad was found, and, in most cases, the company are not mentioned. It is not my intention to belittle any distributor, any advertising medium, or any opportunity by name. Let's just have some fun.

**How to Get 1,000,000 People to Mail You $3. For info, please send $3 to . . .**
Many variations of this common classified ad have appeared. And yes, the trick is to place an ad like this one and hope there are 999,999 more suckers out there (besides yourself).

**No Competition!**
A bold headline on an ad for an MLM long-distance service. There are only about 400 long-distance carriers in the United States, of which roughly 40 are MLM.

**$40,000 Plus a Free Vacation. No Selling—No Recruiting—No Monthly Purchases—No Work of Any Kind!**
And no chance of any kind that it will ever work!

**$320,000 in 18 Months or Less—Results Are Guaranteed . . . Perfectly Legal in Germany!**
"Excuse me Mr. Postal Inspector. You can't touch us U.S. distributors. This program is perfectly legal in Germany!" Yeah, sure. They'll buy that.

**I CAN GET IT IN!**

From an ad run by an advertising agent for an MLM publication. He can get your ad in—get it?

**Earn $90,000 in One Year or More!**

It's funny how a little ol' comma can completely change the meaning of a sentence. By omitting one after the word "Year," this headline essentially says you can earn $90,000 in one or more *years,* not $90,000 or more in one year, as was intended (I hope).

**Build Your Own Downline!**

What a concept!

**Check Out a Company That Does . . . 100% of the Selling . . . 100% of the Recruiting . . . 100% of the Distributors . . . Ask for Darria.**

The company *does* 100% of the distributors? Actually, that is kind of intriguing.

**Cigarettes Go MLM . . . You Won't Lose THIS Downline!!!**

Unless, of course, *they die!*

**Profit!!! No Promises, No Guarantees, No Money Hype.**

The very next line of the ad said "Earn $1,000– $5,000 weekly within 30 days!"
The next line said "No Risk Guarantee."

**No Selling . . . Let the Big Savings Do the Selling for You!**

Has anyone ever seen "big savings" pick up a telephone, call up a prospect, and describe itself?

### Don't Think Your Thoughts. New Thoughts!!!
Huh?

### Ground Floor Opportunity
Attributed to a 130-year-old company that has been operating as an MLM program for more than 20 years.

### Distributors Wanted!
That was the whole ad, plus a phone number. The only thing missing was a reason to call it!

### Pays 100% on Level Six!
That's it. The whole 100% on just the sixth level. Ohhh, look at all the pretty red flags.

### Don't Call This Number!
A recent headline in a display ad. Easy instruction to follow. The ad contained no phone number.

### Hard Work—Great Rewards
What's this? Truth in advertising? In MLM? Better watch out or we just might start signing up only serious, committed people.

### Earn Big Money Working at Home, in Your Mailbox.
Of course, you'll need a reeeeally tiny fax machine, a reeeeally tiny desk . . .

### Amazing New Wealth Secret! Rush S.A.S.E. today!
The system works so well, they require that you spring for the 33¢ stamp to send it to you. Hmmm . . .

### Free Allergies
Sneezing. Watery eyes. Runny nose. And if you act now, they'll even throw in a little athlete's foot!

### I Have Thoroughly Evaluated 2,000-plus MLM Programs . . .

*MarketWave* has spent more than 12,000 man (and woman) hours, over the last 9 years "thoroughly evaluating" MLM opportunities—and we've evaluated about 200.

### You Can Make a Fortune—By Passing Out, or Mailing Tapes I Will Give You.

Passing out seems like less work and a lot more relaxing.

### We Will Place Every Person Who Responds to This Ad After You in Our Downline!

I'm sure *our* should have been *your*. Freudian slip?

### We Do All the Work for You . . . It Is Impossible to Fail.

The funny thing here wasn't so much the text of the ad, but the graphic that accompanied it. Notice that it not only clearly depicts a pyramid shape, but the line goes up, then all the way back down again—just like all downline building schemes do! And 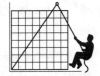 then there's the poor guy dangling vicariously on the right edge, hanging onto the thinner, downward pointing line. There's tons of Freudian stuff going on here.

## The Typo Hall of Fame

### I Earned Over $10.000 in My First 90 Days!

I can make more than that, including tips, working for Domino's Pizza—in my first 90 minutes.

**Credit Problems, Money Troubles, Down On Your Lick?**
That *I* key is just so close to the *U* key, isn't it?

**Join Body Wide Today!**
The real disaster here is that this ad was for a company that sells weight-loss products. Oops!

**History Making MLM Just Lunched!**
No, this wasn't an ad in a magazine, or a card deck, or a promotional flyer. It was the headline on page one of the company's first newsletter!

## Discussion
So . . . what should we be doing (but are not)? It's called proofreading!

\* \* \*

Without a doubt, my most popular Facts & Myths column ever was one of the few that addressed a recruiting technique. Generally, I don't write a lot of how-to material (I tend to focus more on how *not* to), but this particular article just begged to be written.

*MarketWave* was once part of a larger corporation that was headed by three of the most brilliant individuals I have ever met. They had spent many years before my involvement studying and analyzing tons of data they had collected pertaining to what I'll call, for the sake of simplicity, business and sales psychology. My association with these men, and the insights I gained from them, led me to discover a key element in the typical MLM recruiting process that was being completely ignored throughout the industry. And it had nothing to do with MLM, really.

Another element of the recruiting process that I had discovered years earlier (along with several million other network marketers) was one that involved overcoming the MLM stigma. Unfortunately, I found that many distributors were trying to overcome this objection by trying to force their opportunity pitch right through the middle of it. All in the hopes that the features and benefits of their particular program would overcome the prospect's objection to the entire MLM concept. It rarely worked.

These two factors were the inspiration for this article.

## The ABC Technique

WOULD YOU EVER try to pour hot coffee into a thermos with the lid still on? Even with the lid off, could you pour any more in if it was already full? Of course not. Unfortunately, the way that most people prospect for MLM partners makes about as much sense.

For many years, we've all been taught to call up our friends and try to get them to come to an opportunity meeting, or at least read some information or watch a video about our MLM opportunity. To do anything different would be going against the number one commandment of our industry—duplicate what works. In other words, "Thou shalt not try to reinvent the wheel." I'm certainly not about to suggest otherwise. I do, however, believe there are very effective ways of making the wheel roll a little smoother and a little faster.

First and foremost, remember that when you propose your opportunity, you are offering a business opportunity, a chance at being a true entrepreneur. Second, you are proposing that your prospect get involved with multilevel marketing. In other words, you have at least one, and probably two, major challenges. Challenges you must overcome before you can even think about proposing your specific opportunity. Challenges that, 9 times out of 10, are the main reason why your prospect won't even look at your opportunity.

Surveys indicate that about 85% of all working Americans would like to own their own businesses, if they could. In other words, if all obstacles were removed, they would prefer to be their own bosses rather than work for someone else. This amounts to approximately 200 million people! These are your MLM prospects. Now, when 200 million people want to do something and don't do it, there must be a good reason. When they are asked, they answer with the same four reasons every single time:

> **S**urveys indicate that about 85% of all working Americans would like to own their own businesses, if they could.

- It takes too much money. I don't have thousands of dollars to invest in a business.
- It takes too much time. I don't want to work 80 hours a week, 7 days a week to get my business going.
- Too risky. More than 56% of all businesses fail in the first 2 years.[7]
- I don't know how. I've never taken any business courses. I don't know anything about taxes, accounting, marketing, and so on.

---

[7] Small Business Association (1996).

I can assure you, if your prospects are not currently operating their own businesses, they have considered the possibility at some time in their lives. They have also determined all the reasons why they can't (probably all four reasons). Therefore, before you even start to offer your MLM opportunity, you might want to dispel, at least slightly, these beliefs about why they can't go into business for themselves.

Let's say you are having lunch with your friends and you casually mention that you are thinking about starting your own business. Then you ask if they have ever considered it. Sure, they have considered it at some time or another. Well, why didn't you? you ask. They will inevitably respond with one or more of the previous four reasons.

Now comes the fun part. You ask if they would ever consider going into business for themselves if the total start-up costs were under $500 and the income potential was higher than the earnings of some CEOs of Fortune 500 companies; if the total time investment could be as little as 5 to 20 hours a week; if they could continue to work in their present jobs until the income from their business was sufficient to earn at least an equal income, and if they chose to discontinue their business they could return their inventory and marketing materials for as much as a 90% refund (try that with a franchise or conventional business), so there is little risk; and best of all, if there were numerous consultants available who are experts at running this business, who would train and advise them personally, for an unlimited number of hours, for the life of their business, absolutely free! Not only that, you say, but another company will take care of all your research and development, shipping, payroll, sales and payroll taxes, legal questions, and so on. And, this company will do this every month, for the life of their business, for about $25 a year.

Of course, your friends won't believe any of this. Ask your friends if they would consider it if all this were true. Most likely they'll say something like, "Well, sure. But there's got to be a catch." Is there? Isn't this an exact description of your basic MLM opportunity? Is any of this even an exaggeration? No. You've just completed step A of the ABC technique.

Now, for the first time during this conversation, you will suggest that this type of business involves "network" or "multilevel" marketing. But don't get into your specific opportunity yet. There still may be a major hurdle yet to overcome. You still have step B to take care of.

You are going to come across three basic types of people during your recruiting efforts. First, the cynics or skeptics, who believe MLMs are all scams, get-rich-quick schemes, and illegal pyramids; involve door-to-door and home-party sales; and so on. For whatever reason, these people have a low opinion of MLM in general. The second type doesn't know anything about MLM. Perhaps there's some name recognition when you say Amway or Mary Kay, but that's about it. They have no opinion about MLM either way.

The third—unfortunately smallest—group are those who are naturally intrigued by the concept. Usually these people were originally in the second group but heard about someone who made a lot of money doing MLM. By the way, if you find someone in this group, skip step B, which is presenting the MLM concept as a viable, honest form of business. This usually involves explaining what MLM is not, rather than what it is.

You may want to mention that more than 7 million people in the United States are pursuing this form of business. Mention that network marketing is a more than 50-year-old industry that includes more than 1,200 companies. Also, throw out names like Rexall, MCI and US Sprint, Colgate-Palmolive, Gillette, Watkins, and Fuller Brush, which all have MLM divisions or resellers.

Briefly explain the obvious difference between an illegal pyramid and a legitimate MLM company, should this be a concern. In your information package, include favorable articles about the MLM industry in general. You may want to lead with a generic video or audiocassette that explains and legitimizes the industry, rather than promoting any particular opportunity.

So, in step B, you will always do one of two things: define or defend the MLM concept.

Once these first two "preparation" steps are completed, hand your prospect the video or literature about your specific opportunity. If your friends are still skeptical, challenge them to find the catch. Tell them you can't, even though you thought it was too good to be true also. Instead of trying to get them to find out all the good things about your program, encourage them to find all the bad things! Challenge them to debunk it. Let's face it. Someone would be much more likely to watch a video if it were for the purpose of justifying their negative beliefs, rather than contradicting them. It's human nature.

The bottom line is this: The real trick to successful recruiting in any MLM organization is not convincing someone who has looked at your opportunity to get involved with you, it's getting them to just *look* at the opportunity. Don't you agree? Let's face it, once someone seriously looks at a good MLM opportunity, it's pretty hard to not be at least a little intrigued. Unfortunately, 9 out of 10 won't seriously look. If you've got a good opportunity, and you can get them to just *look* at it, the rest will take care of itself.

Like the aforementioned thermos, you must open your prospect's mind before you can pour anything into it. And like the open thermos that's already full, you might have to remove something first. To borrow an analogy from Anthony Robbins (author of the Personal Power program), it's as if your beliefs have legs like a chair. Only these legs are usually solid steel instead of wood. Believe me, people's beliefs about why they can't go into business for themselves, and sometimes what they believe MLM to be, are solid beliefs. If you don't do something to at least weaken those legs before you come in with your new belief, forget it. It will bounce right off.

I'm certainly not suggesting that this ABC technique is going to knock down those legs (although it could). But if you can at least instill some doubt in your prospect's mind, some spark of interest, or at least pessimistic curiosity, you've made a major gain.

I also realize this technique lends itself to certain situations better than others. For example, this technique might be a little more difficult to pull off if you do a lot of long-distance sponsoring. But it's still not impossible. Put it in writing, or better yet, do your own audiotape (with company approval, of course).

Throughout the history of MLM, in almost every MLM organization, we've all been taught to go straight to step C. Contact your prospect and propose your MLM business opportunity. MLM and business can be scary propositions, and needlessly so. Steps A and B are designed to reduce or eliminate this stigma, so you can bring more prospects to step C. Get them to just look!

## Discussion

This article has appeared in seven MLM trade publications, including four that normally refuse previously published works. So I guess there's a lot of perceived value. Unfortunately, I still haven't seen this simple technique incorporated into any company training material. The focus still seems to be almost entirely on getting those who are looking to actually sign up, rather than getting more contacts to just look.

Let's say you contact 100 prospects and 10 actually take a good look at what you're offering. Of those 10, 4 sign up. So 40% of those who looked joined, but only 10% of those contacted looked. Wouldn't it then make more sense to try to increase the number of prospects you bring from step A to step B, rather than trying to improve the already successful process of recruiting those who are looking?

Figure 2.1 shows what would happen to your recruiting numbers if you could get 50% of those contacted to look, even if your actual closing rate of 40% never changed (com-

pared with doubling your closing rate but never getting
more than 10% to look).

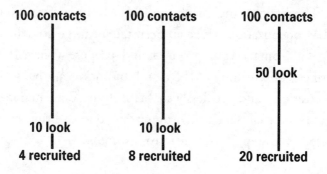

**Figure 2.1** *Increasing recruiting rate versus increasing looking rate.*

Some might say you shouldn't waste your time on people who don't even want to look: Just say "next" and move on. To an extent I agree, but only in the most hopeless situations. Many, possibly most, of the most successful MLMers today likely resisted the concept of MLM when it was first proposed to them. I've heard story after story of people who claimed to have been extremely skeptical of MLM initially, only to have "seen the light" once they seriously considered it.

I firmly believe that the best network marketers in this country aren't involved in network marketing yet. Why? They simply haven't looked close enough.

At the very least, bringing skeptics to the looking stage may not result in a total conversion, but it can dramatically reduce the number of skeptics breeding more skeptics. I think this would make all our jobs a little easier.

Gratuitous plug: Steps A and B of this technique are presented in my cassette tape, "Case Closed! The Whole Truth About Network Marketing." Call 800-688-4766 for details, or visit www.marketwaveinc.com.

\* \* \*

In a way, I suppose it's a good thing that there is so much skepticism by "outer circle" folks, and that existing MLM distributors are so apprehensive about approaching them. As we'll discuss later, in half a century this industry hasn't even approached anything close to a saturation point. If all Americans were to ignore what they've been told

I firmly believe that the best network marketers in this country aren't involved in network marketing yet.

to think, open their minds for a second, clearly and thoroughly evaluate network marketing without prejudice, and actually make their own decision, they'd probably all join!

But it doesn't take a downline organization of tens of thousands to be financially independent. I know many people who earn very comfortable livings with less than 1,500 in their groups. Keep in mind that the term *heavy hitter* is usually reserved for those with 5,000 to 50,000 or more distributors in their downline. So actually, you could be quite successful by sponsoring a half-a-heavy hitter!

Where do you find these super networkers of tomorrow? How can you discover them before they've established themselves with another company? The mega-MLMers are all around you, right here, in . . .

## The Land of 100,000 Unrecruited Heavy Hitters

SEVERAL MONTHS AGO I received a call from one of my downline distributors inquiring about a good "MLM list." Bob then asked specifically if a list of heavy hitters existed and how I might approach them. My response was something to the effect of "Bob, why would you want a list of people who are the least likely to want to join your opportunity?" After all, heavy hitters are people who are making huge monthly incomes (that's why they're called heavy hitters, right?). I'd assume they like making huge monthly incomes and probably would not be too interested in walking away from it and starting over from scratch.

"But Len, think about it," Bob persisted. "Just imagine if I could have recruited. . ." Bob then reeled off the names of three major heavy hitters, all well-known throughout the industry (we'll just call them Mark, Jim, and Ken). Bob began to fantasize about the great wealth to be had by recruiting the likes of even one of the three mega-earners he listed.

Well, I happen to know Mark, Jim, and Ken personally, to varying degrees, and I know their stories. Ironically, all these men claim to have once had a strong skepticism toward network marketing and at one time felt it was something they would never consider being involved in. Yet today, they are three of the richest, most successful network marketers in the country—as are their uplines!

"Exactly!" Bob exclaimed. "So how do we sign up people like that?"

Mark, Jim, and Ken were, at one time, not network marketers, obviously. The lucky folks who personally sponsored these three did not do so by scrolling though existing heavy hitter lists. They worked hard on opening the minds of people who they thought had a lot of potential, got them to consider network marketing, and today are set for life.

You see, about 7 million people are involved in MLM in this country today. About 280 million are not. This means there are literally thousands, perhaps tens of thousands of Marks, Jims, and Kens roaming around this country who, right now, are very skeptical of network marketing, who think they'll never be involved in it—who'll someday make somebody a million-dollar income! Thousands of them!

I think the very best network marketers are not involved in network marketing yet. Mark, Jim, and Ken are only the best out of the 7 million who are involved. The odds are that there are many people among the 280 million who are not network marketers who are far better network marketers than even Mark, Jim, and Ken!

Today, we see a constant ebb and flow of distributors from company to company—those who migrate like gypsies from program to program always looking for the better deal. And this segment of the MLM population is huge. The result is that many companies increase in sales volume and distributor count each month, but it's usually at the expense of another MLM program. Numerous companies that experienced growth in the '90s benefited primarily from the fallout of other MLM companies.

Really, no company has experienced legitimate momentum in the last half of the '90s. Not like Herbalife in 1983,

NSA from 1987 to 1988, NuSkin in 1991, or Cell Tech in 1994. Or, to a lesser extent, Quorum and Melaleuca in 1992 and 1993, respectively. The point is that these companies created this momentum by bringing in massive numbers of new distributors from *outside* the industry. And as a result, the industry grew as well.

But not today, at least not like in the 1980s and very early 1990s. Today, everybody seems to be into retreading existing distributors over and over and dreaming about landing the big heavy hitter. The industry has become sluggish and lazy, filled with a lot of spoiled opportunists looking for something for as close to nothing as possible. And the opportunities available to them have exploited and perpetuated this to no end. Where there was once an industry composed of merit-based opportunities that rewarded those who worked hard, retailed, and actually trained and supported their downline, there is now an industry full of fluff programs with token products that will basically sell you the farm for a small monthly personal purchase (certainly not all are like this—there are still many "traditional" opportunities as well, you just have to look a lot harder to find them). Again, the point is that recruiting outer circle people (those not involved in MLM) is hard work, and so few MLMers today are into working hard.

Why is it so hard? Because outer circle recruitment involves a two- and usually three-phase process—and the first two steps are very tough ones.

Remember the ABC technique? Step A is to open the prospects' minds to starting their own businesses. Even the idea of a simple "home-based" business might still conjure the four major dreads of most would-be entrepreneurs (too much money, too much time, too much risk, not enough knowledge, experience, or confidence). Step B is to overcome the concerns or apprehensions your prospects might have toward network marketing in general. Step C is when you finally present your particular MLM opportunity—if you can get to step C.

So, wouldn't it be so much easier to just find folks who are already involved in MLM, who've already gotten past these first two steps, and just convince them that your products are better and your compensation plan will pay them more? Steps A and B can be tough, so why go through all the trouble of taking new people through these steps when you can go after an existing MLM participant? That way, someone else has already done the tough part for you!

Because, if you don't, this industry will not grow, your downline will be forever turning over as these transient MLMers move on to the next better deal, and you will never recruit a heavy hitter!

There are thousands of them out there. Get out there and recruit one. Just *one!*

## Discussion

You might get the idea that everyone who is not involved in network marketing has some type of aversion toward it. Actually, I've found that most of the time step B is a snap simply because most people don't have any opinion about MLM at all. Many have yet to even hear about it! Again, I believe this is a result of participants within the industry only talking it up within the industry.

A few years ago I decided to travel across the country by train. I'd never been on a train, I was in no hurry to get to where I was going (to work in the home office of an MLM company), and the idea of having nothing to do for 3 days was delightful. During meals all the passengers sat in the dining car in groups of four. Rarely did I sit with the same person more than once. During these meals three questions would inevitably be asked of each person at the table: Where are you from, where are you going, and what do you do?

Each time it was my turn to describe my occupation (I like to use the term "professional network marketer") the response would be—every time—something to the effect of, "What's that?" And each time I described what I did in more detail, I was astounded to find that my dining partners didn't have a clue what I was talking about! Oh, sure, when I'd mention Amway or Mary Kay, there was usually some recognition of the name, but little more. And, keep in mind that most of the Amtrak passengers were older than 50. They had lived longer than there has been an MLM industry—yet had never been introduced to it.

Pretty exciting, isn't it?

\* \* \*

Another article I wrote about just getting prospects to look came after I had attended a seminar conducted by a Tony Robbins wannabe (much of his material came directly from Robbins's Personal Power tapes, in some cases verbatim) who was attempting to bestow the virtues of NLP (neuro-linguistic programming) technology on a room full of MLM distributors. About the only thing he mentioned (this was an all-day event) that even remotely lent itself to building a successful downline, which was the premise of the presentation, involved discovering your prospects' "hot buttons." In other words, what do they really want to hear that is specific to their personal agendas.

I had already been doing some research into this question, and it was already glaringly obvious to me that money was not the primary motivation of most MLM distributors or their prospects. At least, great wealth was not. It was always something else. This article addresses what most prospects want, how you can discover the real needs and desires of your prospects, and how to incorporate this vital information into the process of bringing more people to the looking stage.

## What Do Your Prospects *Really* Want?

EVERYBODY WANTS MONEY, right? Money, money, money! Of course you know what your prospects want. What a stupid question. They all want more M-O-N-E-Y. How do you get them to join your multilevel opportunity? Why, just tell them how much money they'll make. Join our program and you could make this much money. Sure, there may be other reasons, but the main, primary, overriding motivation is always going to be to the gobs of money you can make, right?

Wrong.

Think about this. If you had 50,000 $20 bills in front of you right now (that's a million dollars), is it really what you want? It is? Then why would you go out and exchange all of it for something else? In other words, you would spend it. Because it's not the money that people really want, it's all the stuff they can get with the money!

So the question you need to ask is, if my prospect had the money, what would he or she get with it? That's what your prospect *really* wants. Then proceed to explain how your opportunity can be the vehicle to acquire it. The end, not the means.

Granted, telling someone he or she could earn a million dollars with your opportunity can still be a fairly powerful, albeit misleading, motivator, but it's just so . . . cliché. Everybody says you can get rich in his or her program.

If you knew, for example, that your prospect wanted a bigger house, and a new boat, and liked to fish, you could describe to him pulling up to the pier in the back of his huge, new home after an afternoon of fishing at his favorite lake. Of course, mention that he caught lots of fish.

If you knew someone who liked to ski and wanted a new car, don't tell her how much money she could make; tell her this could be a way she could drive to the mountains in her brand new BMW. Ski rack included.

What if your prospects are strangers, and you don't know these things about them? Just ask. Ask them simply: Why is it that you may be interested in getting involved in an opportunity like this? Don't assume anything. If their answer is vague, explore a little. Ask straight out, if you have to: What would you want out of this venture?

Naturally, they'll probably respond by saying they want to make money. But guess what. Of the more than 6,000 people we surveyed, the vast majority didn't say money! As a matter of fact, they didn't mention any material gain at all.

What they wanted was either "security" or "more free time." And when those who did say they wanted more money were asked why, about half responded with the same type of answer. More time, freedom, security, sense of accomplishment, recognition, and respect were common responses.

**T**he majority of your prospects don't want more money, or even the material things it can be exchanged for, but rather the feelings they get by possessing money.

What all this boils down to is this: The majority of your prospects don't want more money, or even the material things it can be exchanged for, but rather the feelings they get by possessing money. When it comes to persuasion techniques, knowing what those feelings are can be an extremely powerful tool. And a dangerous one, if used unethically.

So you asked them what they want, and they said money. You asked them why, and they said they wanted more free time. If you can take this one step further and find out why they want more free time, then you've really got something to work with. Let's say your prospect describes a situation where he feels he's neglected his family. He just doesn't spend enough quality time with his wife and kids like he should. Or, maybe he wants to quit his job because he hates getting up at 5 A.M. and commuting for an hour. Describe, in vivid detail, how your opportunity could allow him to sleep in, work at home, be with his family, and so on, and you'll find many more prospects at least looking at your opportunity.

One last, but crucial, point. This can be powerful stuff. It should be used only to get your prospects to look at your offer. It should not be used to get them to actually sign up! This is not a closing technique. The final decision must be your prospect's, and it must be based on clear-headed, realistic expectations.

Notice how liberally I used the word "could" when suggesting the responses you might give your prospects. Suggest that your opportunity "could" provide them with whatever they're seeking. Don't imply that it "will" or even "should" solve their problems. Be realistic.

I am a very strong advocate of doing whatever it takes to get otherwise skeptical or disinterested prospects to at least consider MLM as a legitimate and worthwhile venture. This type of persuasion technique can be one way to help accomplish this. But don't defeat the purpose. Be sure you make clear to your prospects, at some point between looking and booking, that you are only offering the vehicle, and they still have to drive it. And it's not an automatic!

## Discussion

I recently spoke at a national kickoff for a new MLM company. I started my presentation by saying, "How many people here would like to learn how to make $250,000 per month, within 6 to 18 months from today?" The response was less than enthusiastic. Oh, there was a smattering of applause, a few hoots and cheers, a couple hands raised, but mostly a lot of bad body language (furrowed brows, crossed arms). Someone even hissed and booed. I quickly explained to them that I was being facetious, and that this was not the type of ridiculous hype they were going to hear that afternoon. Those with their arms crossed relaxed. Those with their hands up sheepishly crossed their arms.

Later in that same presentation, I used one of the best hot button lines I've ever heard. I asked them to imagine what it would feel like to wake up in the morning and absolutely know that all their bills will be paid this month whether they "roll out of bed—or roll over." This time I got a rousing ovation. They went nuts! These people were actually more excited about the idea of sleeping in than they were about making a quarter-million bucks a month!

I don't know who originated this "or roll over" line, but I would like to thank that person. It's the line that moved me to get back into network marketing. And all of you who have ever called my office before 10 A.M. only to get my answering machine—now you know why.

Before we leave this subject, I do want to make one more comment about these persuasion techniques in relation to selling an MLM opportunity.

One of the persuasion techniques that I see taught at MLM training events involves what they call "mirroring and modeling." This is where you subtly mimic the mannerisms of your prospect. If they tap their feet a lot, you tap your foot a lot. If they like to hold pencils in one hand and scratch their heads with the other, you grab a pencil and start scratching your head. The result is that they will subconsciously create an attachment to you. They'll just like you more! After all, we all tend to be attracted to people who are like us, right?

Another similar technique involves watching your prospects' eye movements as they speak. If their eyes look up a lot, they're "visual" people. Side to side means they are "auditory" people. Down? Those are "feeling" people. So if they tend to look up a lot, you're suppose to start peppering your conversation with visual connotations, such as "I see" or "Visualize if you will . . . " or "Take a look at this . . . " Again the result is that they will become more comfortable and feel closer to you.

Actually, this stuff works! I've tried it and it's almost scary what can happen. But the real question is this: Do you really *want* it to work with an MLM prospect? Maybe to move some product, sure. But remember that these techniques are being taught to recruit new distributors!

So let's say your prospect isn't really interested in your opportunity. So you start mirroring and modeling. You're tapping your foot, rubbing your nose. You start saying things like, "I really mean this from the *heart,* John. I really *feel* like you're *emotionally* ready for this *euphoric* opportunity!" Your prospect looks down a lot, you see. Suddenly, he just loves you and everything you're telling him. He signs up. The next morning, he calls you up and says (while looking down, of course) "I'm just not that *excited* about this anymore. I *feel* like I've made the wrong decision." What are you going to do? Run over to their house, start rubbing your nose and tapping your foot, look down at the floor and say, "I don't understand your *feelings* about this, John. I'm really *depressed* that I didn't properly convey the *joy* of working this business. I would *love* for you to reconsider, and *feel* that. . . . " Give me a break. The best persuasion technique in the world is a fair compensation plan, a solid, honest company, and a quality product line.

It's a simple business, folks. You don't have to be a master persuader to succeed. Just get your prospect to look.

* * *

So . . . how *do* you close a prospect? That was the question I decided to deal with in the following article. In this case, I had just witnessed a top distributor for a major MLM company (he actually was pulling in almost a quarter-million dollars a month at the time) doing a training session at a local hotel. Part of the day was spent on closing techniques. They were the same stock closing lines they teach those telemarketers who try to sell you resort memberships or personalized pens. It was pretty pathetic to watch.

> The best persuasion technique in the world is a fair compensation plan, a solid, honest company, and a quality product line.

## The Perfect Close

WHEN IT COMES to the philosophy of MLM recruiting, the techniques and strategies are as wide and varied as the people involved in the industry. There are all kinds of suggested ways of finding a good company, locating leads, introducing your opportunity, getting people to opportunity meetings, conducting the formal presentation, and closing the prospect.

I believe that there really is no definitive right or wrong way of performing any of the latter steps in building your MLM organization. The success or failure of many of those ways depends, for the most part, on intangibles that only the individual distributor can determine. Who knows what's really the best way for Mary to cold call? Or for John to conduct a presentation? Much depends on Mary and John's personalities, attitudes, motivation, and communication skills and the nature of their particular opportunities.

But when it comes to closing techniques, we really only advocate one method—across the board. It's a simple technique that will practically guarantee you an active, healthy downline and a dramatically reduced attrition rate within your organization. And it's not that tough to pull off.

Enough suspense. When you've got your prospects at the stage of decision, when they've exhausted every last question, when it's time for the rubber to hit the road (when the pen hits the distributor application), and you're ready to spring that brilliant closing technique on them you learned at last weekend's training workshop . . . don't! Forget the "double yes close" or the "momentum close." Don't even think about trying the "assumptive close." Try, instead, something brilliant like this: "So Cathy, are you ready to start?" Or perhaps something really clever like, "So, Frank, what do you think? Do you want to get started?" Or maybe even something a little bolder like: "Let's go for it! What do you say?"

I know you are probably thinking it must have taken me years of research and field testing to come up with such incredible closes. But seriously . . .

What I'm obviously saying here is, *don't* close them. The prospects must close themselves! Let me explain.

We must put this whole MLM recruitment thing in perspective. Assuming the prospects are getting into this business to be successful, which would obviously be a safe assumption, then what are we really selling them here? No, not a used car, not life insurance, not a piece of real estate, but a livelihood! A means to earn a living. A way of life!

What is the true definition of a close? In my opinion, it is the artificial creation of, and inducement into, a decision. In other words, you did or said something that created a motivation, a feeling, that may not have been there naturally. If this is so, your new recruits will most likely go home, go to sleep, wake up the next morning and say, "Why did I do that?" And they'll have to be "closed" all over again. And again and again.

Even worse, you may have psychologically persuaded them to get into something that they believed to be of more value to them personally than perhaps it really is. You may have closed them on the idea that your opportunity is something a little more than it really is, just to get them in. And a few weeks later, when they find out the truth, they can feel deceived or misled.

What we really need to look for are those people who will go home at night and can't sleep. Someone who will interrupt you near the end of your presentation and ask, "So how do I get started?" Even if you have to use one of the non-closes offered earlier, you will at least leave it up to your prospects to make the final decision. And it will, hopefully, be their decision. Created naturally in their own minds, based solely on their own values, motives, and desires.

I do advocate doing whatever you can to get prospects to look at your opportunity (such as the ABC technique). Looking never hurt anybody. But understand that getting them to look is completely different from getting them to sign up and actually pursue the business once they've looked. And, of course, you may have to eventually close the prospect on the idea of making a decision. Any decision . . . yes or no.

Sure, using this type of non-close can reduce your recruiting ratio a little. But what's the alternative? If you really want to just put people through the treadmill, get a few quick hits of product volume before they drop out, fine. Tell them whatever they want to hear. Just get their names on the dotted line. Throw the mud against the wall and see what sticks.

If, however, you're looking for some good, committed, serious people, let them show you who they are. You'll know when you find them. Sure, this can make your job a little harder. But nobody ever closed you by telling you this was going to be easy . . . did they?

## Discussion

This article was actually kind of an ego buster. I thought I had some new and wonderful insight that the MLM world sorely needed to hear—only to discover that people like Tom "Big Al" Schreiter, Randy Gage, John Kalench, and many more had been advocating the non-close for years.

I guess great minds do think alike!

* * *

I made a point earlier in "The Perfect Close" that I like to expound on in my live seminars. There is no definitive right or wrong way of doing this business that applies to every distributor. Unfortunately, I've read quite a bit of material that suggests otherwise.

Take, for example, the issue of width versus depth. One very prominent networker and author advocates width pretty much universally (placing all your recruits on your first level). Another I know feels that depth is the only way to go (placing most of your recruits under each other). Well, how well do you think the width argument is going to fly with a distributor in a $2 \times 12$ matrix program (2 wide, 12 levels deep) or a binary (which prohibits more than 2 people on the first level)? Would you advise building deep in a breakaway program that requires 16 first-level, personally sponsored break-away groups to achieve the highest commissions?

What about the argument over which to lead with: the product or the opportunity? If your next door neighbor is speaking to you from over the hedge, and she says "You know, Jane, I'm thinking about starting a home business. I need some extra money," are you going to respond, "Who cares, Karen. Let me tell you about this great shampoo I'm using." Or, if she tells you, "My skin is so dry. I need to try a new brand of moisturizer," are you going say, "Life's a drag, Karen. But I'll bet some extra money might cheer you up, huh?"

Okay, I'm exaggerating, a little. But do you see the point? There is no universal right or wrong answer to these debates. Personally, I'm a depth guy. But that's what works best for the program I work, those I work with, and my own agenda. Not having any idea what situation you're in, I wouldn't dare suggest that you should do what I do. The same with what to lead with. I believe you get investors with a company, customers with a product, and distributors with a comp plan—the fact that you need all three to be successful notwithstanding. These would just be my priorities depending on who I was talking to and their personal situations. Be flexible. Play it by ear. Once you get to talking with your prospect you'll know which approach to take.

One other common debate has been raging for years: When is the best time to get involved in an MLM opportunity? I addressed this issue at length in the month just before "The Perfect Close" article.

## MLM Strategies—Ground Floor or Momentum?

ONE OF THE MANY controversies surrounding MLM "theory" is determining the optimum time to get involved with an opportunity. Prelaunch, ground floor, right before or just after the momentum phase begins, after the company growth stabilizes, maturity . . . who knows for sure? There are pros and cons to getting involved in each stage of a company's growth.

First of all, forget prelaunch. There's no such thing. Either you launched or you didn't. Either you're accepting applications, moving product, and paying commissions, or you're not. The term *prelaunch* is a marketing gimmick to make the opportunity sound really ground floor.

The major problem with getting involved with ground floor opportunities is that they are usually no more than one story high. Most start-up MLMs are long gone before the ink dries on their brochures. Hard data (see "MLM Start Ups . . ." article) suggests there really is a more than 95% failure rate among MLM start-ups within the first 24 months (for years it was just an assumed figure).

Another drawback to start-up operations is the lack of a sophisticated support base. When you try to go upline to get advice and support from those already successful in the business, and you reach the president of the company just two levels above you, where do you go? Few start-ups will provide video- and audiotapes, or at least good ones, right out of the chute. And how do you hold a convincing opportunity meeting with two people? You need a track to run on. There must be successful predecessors for you to duplicate. A ground floor opportunity has no predecessors, successful or otherwise. Everyone's starting from scratch.

Even if the company does make it through that treacherous first year, you still may have to wait another year or two or three or four (or more) before any real substantial growth occurs. This stage is usually called the momentum phase, when name recognition starts to kick in and the geometric expansion of the organization really starts to explode. Well then, the best time to get in would be right before this momentum stage hits (it's just so obvious, isn't it?). Oh, and the best horse to bet on is the one that's going to come in first, the best stock to buy is the one that's about to go up, and the best person to marry is someone who's about to win $10 million in the lottery in a community property state. But, alas, this would all require a crystal ball, of course (or a good 900 psychic line).

When a company is about to go into momentum is totally speculative. Naturally, most young companies like to think, and will try to convince you, that they are on the brink of momentum. I've heard a company claim they were into momentum 4 days after they launched! In fact, I don't know of a single company that isn't going into momentum soon, allegedly.

Okay, so how about right after momentum hits? Some will say that's too late. That may even appear to be true, since a good indicator of when a company is in momentum is when everybody seems to be doing it. The saturation myth starts to take over. But if this logic were correct, then momentum would cease. Yet, momentum phases sometimes last many months, or even years. Some, though, are short-lived and weak, and some never really occur at all.

> **W**hen a company is about to go into momentum is totally speculative. Naturally, most young companies like to think, and will try to convince you, that they are on the brink of momentum.

And, by the way, this stage of an MLM company's growth cycle can also be crippling, or even fatal. Many times a company is not ready for it and can't keep up, and those who anticipate it may have to go into heavy debt since the revenues are not there yet (in fact, any company that claims to be debt-free and in momentum is likely fibbing about one or the other). There is a big difference between an MLM company keeping up and catching up. It's usually the difference between life and death for the company. Once an MLM operation going into momentum gets even 1 month behind the growth curve, it's like letting go of the reins of a wild horse. Forget it. It's gone.

Keeping up means staying ahead of the growth curve. This means upgrading the computer system, adding more phone lines, hiring more employees, advance-ordering more inventory, perhaps moving to larger facilities, and all this usually occurs during the worst possible time—momentous growth! It's like changing a tire at 60 miles per hour. That's why it's not unusual to find companies using the terms *momentum* and *growing pains* in the same presentation.

Let's discuss this momentum stuff in a bit more detail. This stage is actually a normal part of the growth cycle of any kind of business, only the upward curve of the graph tends to be much more acute, and the increase in sales more dramatic, in an MLM operation because of the geometric expansion of the sales force.

I firmly believe that the whole MLM industry will someday go into a momentum phase. With more and more people wanting to work at home, or who are not working at all, this alternative form of income will become more and more intriguing. And with the technologies we have today that lend themselves to this business so well, such as fax machines, voice mail, conference calling, videos, satellite communication, the Internet, and so on, it will be an even easier (relatively) business to pursue. I think that this industry momentum will result in companies hitting their momentum sooner and the momentum lasting longer.

Not only do companies go into momentum, but indi
vidual downlines do as well. Eventually, if you stay with it
long enough, this geometric progression will kick in for
your specific downline. After all, it is just a mini version of
a company downline.

Figure 2.2 reveals that this upward growth could occur
at all three levels, to approximately the same degree. The
only difference is that the industry growth is measured in
decades, the company growth in years, and your personal
organization growth in months.

So let's see . . . start-up is too risky and takes too long,
premomentum is too speculative, postmomentum may be
too late and can also be very risky—how about we just play
it safe, be a little conservative, and get involved with a well-
established, middle-aged company that is just reaching its
peak? Let's think about this.

There are basically three different stages, or tests,
through which an MLM company must pass before it can
really be considered "safe." One is start-up, which we've

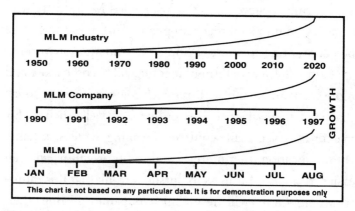

**Figure 2.2** *Geometric progression (momentum) can occur
within any size downline organization*

discussed. Two is momentum, which has its poisons as well. Three is the scrutiny phase. This phase usually occurs when a company is near its peak—when its distributor base is at its highest. This is also when their P-O total is at its highest.

A company's P-O factor represents the percentage of its total distributor base, both active and inactive, who are P-O'd! Unfortunately, government regulatory agencies and the media don't go by the percentage, they go by raw totals. You could have a company with one million distributors and a 1% P-O factor, and another company with only 1,000 distributors and a 90% P-O factor, and guess which one will get ripped in the media and attacked by attorney generals? The big guy. They've got 10,000 P-O'd people, whereas that little sleazy rip-off company only has 900.

So getting in right at the peak, or just after momentum, can drop you right into the middle of the battlefield.

Some examples of companies that are victims of this test are United Sciences of America (deceased), FundAmerica (the Elvis of MLM, dead but there are still sightings), Herbalife (passed), Amway (passed), Mary Kay (passed), NuSkin (passed), American Gold Eagle (reincarnated into Gold Unlimited—which didn't pass), NSA (passed), Jewelway (gone), Holiday Magic (long gone), International Heritage (gone), and many, many more. Some who have made it through get set back and may have to face this stage again.

So what does this mean? Is it best to get involved with an old, mature company? Sure, it could work, but then you have to deal with the perception of saturation. And that's not counting the many hundreds of thousands of ex-distributors these older companies have racked up the last 20 or 30 years.

So what exactly are we saying here? Never get involved with an MLM company? Not at all. The real question you should ask is, What's best for you?

All phases of a company's growth have their advantages and disadvantages (you'll hear about all the advantages at the opportunity meeting—I'm just trying to balance the scale a little). Your risk factor increases the earlier you get in, but so does your income potential. You could label MLMers the same way you label investors. Conservative? Find a well-established company past the scrutiny stage. Aggressive? Go for ground floor. Or, are you somewhere in between? Only you have the answer.

The bottom line is this: Any business venture has its risks. MLM included. Just pick the best opportunity for you, in a company that you feel comfortable with. Commit to it, work hard at it, and be honest and ethical at all times. If you and your organization can do these things, you will greatly increase your company's chances of being there for you in the long run.

## Discussion

Width versus depth, product versus opportunity, and when to get involved are just a few of the strategy debates. There are many more.

Should you try to recruit long distance or only from your center of influence? There are so many factors involved in answering this one I won't try to list them all. First, how much time and money do you have to invest? Long-distance sponsoring can get pretty costly. How many MLM programs have you been in before? In other words, do you have any center of influence left?

Personally, I'd go with the standard theory that your warmest contacts (best friends, family, and so on) are a great place to start. Sure, you'll probably spend most of your time listening to them try to talk you out of it rather than talking them into it, but so what? These leads are free! At least if they say no thanks, you didn't waste any money. Some MLM authorities might suggest you only pursue your friends and family after you've achieved some degree of success. But that could create a catch-22. There are so many people who became successful *by* approaching their warm market first. By not doing so, you may be making it harder to achieve the success you feel you first need before approaching them. Besides, if you instead work the cold market via direct mail, ad co-ops, or however, you'll still be approaching friends and family—just someone *else's*.

There are so many factors to consider. I'd be a fool to blindly tell you which recruiting approach to take without knowing you.

Should you inventory product? Should you hold opportunity meetings? Should you have home parties?

Yes—if you want to retail tons of products. But you know what? Tons of folks don't want to retail any products. They just want to personally consume their volume each month. I love doing meetings. Many MLMers today don't even want to attend them. But, many still do.

What type of plan should you join? Breakaway? Binary? Unilevel or matrix? Should the qualifications be high or low? Should the payout be strongest at the early stages of the plan, or should the commissions be loaded on the back end? All are good questions, and ones that no one can answer for you. It depends on what you're after. Low-qualifying plans, or plans with the greatest payout on the first two or three levels, tend to spread the commissions around more. More earn a few hundred dollars per month, but no one ever gets rich. A high-qualifying, back-end heavy plan will increase your chances of becoming a millionaire, but there can be some long, hard, and very lean times along the way. No plan can completely satisfy both ends of the spectrum (I don't care how many say so). Which end would you be satisfied with? Or are you somewhere in between?

**Like any legitimate business, you should first lay out your objectives. You should create a business plan.**

Defining MLM strategy is like trying to generically define "business strategy" without even knowing what kind of business we're talking about.

Like any legitimate business, you should first lay out your objectives. You should create a business plan. After you are very clear about the various questions that have been posed here, and you know exactly what you are after, you can begin to define the strategy necessary to achieve those goals.

* * *

I'm currently developing a live presentation based on my antihype campaign that I hope to market to all legitimate MLM companies. It's designed to teach distributors how to remain competitive and still be honest and realistic. It focuses on how one might combat the hype being used against them by a competitor without crossing the line into competition bashing. I think this is the right spot in this book to give you a little sneak preview. It's definitely part of an effective recruiting strategy that we *should* be doing, but for the most part are not.

For now, the seminar has the working title . . .

## MLM Defense

IN PRACTICALLY EVERY competitive endeavor, whether sports, business, law, politics, or even, one could argue, life, there are two forces that we summon to defeat our opponent. We offer up an offense and a defense. In most types of sports the delineation between, and the need for each, is obvious. Take away the defensive players from any football team and you will lose every contest, no matter how many touchdowns you score. Baseball, hockey, basketball, and many other sports all involve points for and against. In some sports defense is the key element. Eliminate defense from professional boxing and you'd have very short boxing matches and very few professional boxers, at least, ones who can still feed themselves. In business, advertisers don't always tell us just why we should buy their brand, but they often include reasons we should not buy a competitor's brand. In law, defense is paramount since the burden of proof is on the prosecution (the offense) and all the defense has to do is create a slight doubt in the minds of the jury.

In politics I consider offense to be the presentation of all the reasons why a candidate should be elected. Political defense would be, as in sports, the attempt to impede the progress of an opponent. Not only is this a key element of any election process, but some candidates seem to base their entire campaign on why you shouldn't vote for the other candidate, rather than why you should vote for themselves.

And, yes, one could make a case that there is an offensive and defensive aspect to practically every decision we make in our daily lives. Every decision, no matter how small, is designed to either avoid pain or gain pleasure. We naturally tend to move toward what we desire and away from what we detest, the proverbial "carrot and the stick." In this case both the offense and the defense are within us. You offer them both (à la the devil and angel sitting on each shoulder) and base your decision on who wins the debate.

Let's try an experiment, right now. I'm going to describe the occupation of an individual and I want you to visualize that person in an action pose. Don't think about it, just note the first image that pops in your mind. Ready?

Football player. Basketball player. Boxer. Soldier in combat. You, looking at a big slice of your favorite flavor of cake.

Now, think back. Were the images offensive or defensive? Did you picture a quarterback ready to throw a pass or a fullback running with the ball? The vast majority do (I've performed this test many times before). Was the basketball player taking a shot (almost always) or blocking the shot (almost never)? Was the boxer throwing a punch? I've never, ever, had someone tell me they visualized a guy cowering in the corner with his gloves covering his face. Was the soldier in attack mode, or was he crouched in a fox hole? Did you see yourself looking at the cake wide-eyed and drooling, or head turned away with arms outstretched, shunning the temptation? Come on, be honest.

Although defense is a vital part of practically every aspect of our lives, we are certainly an offensive-focused society. We want to score points, not prevent them. And we want to score a lot of them.

So, what is MLM defense? Unfortunately, it is, at least currently, a lot like political defense. As more and more candidates devote more and more time to mud slinging and self-serving hype, so are network marketers. And as more and more disillusioned Americans vote "none of the above" at the polls, our MLM prospects are reacting in much the same way.

What MLM defense *should* be, and what it hardly ever is or is ever taught to be, is a dignified, professional, factual presentation of the benefits that your MLM program has over a specific competitor, and the debunking of alleged benefits posed by your competition when those benefits are, in fact, exaggerated or illusionary.

Hype is a primary tool in the recruiting process of many, and arguably *most*, network marketers today. Almost every prospect you contact will be evaluating other opportunities as well as yours. Therefore, you have *opponents* in this process, and they may not play fair. They may relate bogus or even slanderous information to your prospect about your opportunity (more on that later) or positive information about their own program that may involve some degree of hype. If you can *defend* against this and at the same time offer a powerful offense (what's good about your opportunity), then you have *twice* as powerful a presentation. While you're scoring points, you're preventing your opponent from scoring. It's like a scale. Doesn't it make sense that you'd have a far better chance of tipping the scale in your favor if you not only added weight to your side but legitimately removed weight from the other?

When an opponent is hyping your prospect, you have three options: (1) Ignore the opponent and continue to present a hype-free, realistic depiction of the benefits of your MLM program—and take the risk of losing the prospect to the hype; (2) have a hype contest to see who can outhype whom, and even if you win your prospects will discover the truth eventually and end up just as much *not* in your downline as if they hadn't enrolled in the first place (only now they walk away feeling scammed), or (3) stick to your honest, realistic presentation about your company and *defend* yourself against the hype.

I realize there's sometimes a fine line between an honorable MLM defense and gratuitous competition bashing. The best way to audit yourself is to ask this simple question: Can I prove my statement? In other words, are you saying something you can be accountable for? Can you back it up? For example, if a competitor claims his or her plan "pays infinitely deep," you should be able to prove both mathematically and logically that this claim is completely false. Don't go so far as to suggest that infinity bonuses are wrong or bad, because they are not. Just explain why they aren't *as good* as your competition is claiming. Or, what if your prospect is impressed by huge income claims made by a competing distributor? There's a whole section later in this book on how to defend against this, but for now just know that you can and must defend against it. Don't allow your prospect to be swayed by meaningless information. Force your competition to stick to the *genuine* merits of their opportunity.

You can also use this same "proof" question as a defensive weapon. For example, if someone tells your prospects that they shouldn't join your company because "they're going down," or "nobody's making any money," or "they're being investigated," ask your prospect to ask your competitor this question: "Would you please put that in writing and sign your name?" Then watch them backpedal! When they refuse (which they *always* will), ask your prospect why they wouldn't do this if they were certain of their claim? Demand that they be accountable for their derogatory remarks. Demand that they reveal *how they know* what they are saying it true. Of course, they rarely can, which not only greatly diminishes the impact of their mud slinging but can dramatically reduce the credibility of *everything* they say.

I could try to give you more examples of statements you could defend against, but I won't. First of all, this book is chock full of them already! Second, I've already summarized practically every MLM pitch ever given earlier in this book. Remember? "We have the best products . . . the best support system . . . the most lucrative compensation plan . . . and the company is debt free and about to go into momentum." That's it. Now, when I suggested that you then ask your prospect to ask your competitors, "How do you know?" that's MLM defense.

If you're going to back up your claims about your company, then you have every right to demand the same from your competition.

* * *

What do you do on a 7-hour flight to Orlando when you've already seen the movie and the person sitting next to you doesn't speak English? You sit and think. Being a 41-year-old, childless bachelor, I spent the first three hours thinking about my social life and raising a family (or more specifically, the dream of finally having the time to have one of each). Being a professional network marketer, I spent the next three hours thinking about network marketing. Being a writer who had to come up with a column by that Friday, I decided to spend the last hour thinking about both.

> **I**f you're going to back up your claims about your company, then you have every right to demand the same from your competition.

The result is as follows:

## Courting MLM: Are We Ever Going to Get Married?

IN MANY UNFORTUNATE ways, the correlation between human courtship and the way in which many of us play the field within MLM is disturbingly similar. In other ways, it is not similar enough. An analysis of how our species seeks out mates compared with how we decide on which MLM opportunity to commit to might reveal a lot about the MLM condition in this country.

Let's take a look.

First, let's evaluate the four basic components of what we look for in a potential mate. First, there's physical appearance. Not just facial features and body characteristics but style and dress as well. Second, there's personality. How easy is this person to get along with? How much does he or she have in common with your world view? Is he or she emotionally stable? How supportive and respectful is he or she? In general, how likable is this person? Third, at least in most cases, is the degree of this person's success. How much money does this person make? How much security does he or she offer? And the fourth and final consideration is that totally intangible, mysterious thing we call love. Which, by the way, most would agree has nothing whatsoever to do with items 1 through 3.

So what basic components do we look for in a good MLM opportunity? I could answer that question by essentially reiterating the entire previous paragraph, making only a few minor word changes.

Certainly the overall appearance, or perception, we have of an MLM program is key. MLM is by far the most perception-oriented business opportunity in this country. Especially when it comes to compensation plans. Who cares what it really pays—how good does it look on paper? That is, unfortunately, what seems to count most.

Does a company's "personality" make a difference? Have you ever been involved with or considered an MLM opportunity that didn't appreciate or respect its distributors? Was unstable? Had little in common with your philosophy or product interest? Just wasn't very likable?

Some folks may claim that level of success or amount of wealth is not a consideration when it comes to a mate (and most of them would be fibbing, at least to themselves), but it would be foolish to claim this makes no difference in picking an MLM program to commit to. It is a major consideration.

Even "love" comes into play.

I've found so little difference between the symptoms of love and infatuation, at least in the beginning. I've had crushes that I would swear were cases of true love. Only after years of experience and growth do we finally gain the maturity to tell the two apart (remember our grade school days when we were in love with every good-looking boy or girl in our class?).

Both infatuation (crush) and love can make us swoon, not eat or sleep for days, distract us, obsess us, make us act real goofy, temporarily enhance our efforts to look and act better than we normally do, and just get us all excited. The difference is that one stays and the other goes away. It's like two mountains. Time may weather away one mountain and turn it into nothing. There's nothing solid underneath to support it. Or, it could be like one of those volcanic mounds you see in Arizona landscapes where the loose, soft dirt washes away, but there's a strong, rock-solid core that will remain for centuries. In the beginning, from the outside, they both look pretty much the same.

Same with MLM opportunities.

Have you ever fallen in love with an MLM opportunity at first sight? Have you ever gone to a meeting or heard a presentation for the first time and left 3 feet in the air? Not been able to sleep that night? Got all excited and distracted? Has an MLM opportunity ever made you act at least a little goofy? (Be honest, now.)

Then, usually, it goes away, doesn't it? The novelty, the infatuation, the crush dissolves into nothing. And sometimes, usually after months or even years of searching, you find one that—oh, perhaps you lose a little passion for it after a while—you get comfortable with. It works (always a good trait in a mate), it's supportive, it doesn't cheat, so you get complacent. And then, in those oh-so-rare and glorious, perhaps once-in-a-lifetime moments, you find one you fall head over heels in love with. And no power on earth will ever pry you away from that MLM program.

The comparisons are endless.

Ever fallen in love with an MLM program and then gotten dumped? Ouch! I swear it's the same kind of pain. It's awful. It eats you up inside thinking about the "possibilities," the lost promise, the fear of never finding another quite like that one.

Ever fallen in love with an MLM program and then settled down and had a family? You bet we have. That's exactly what MLM is all about, isn't it? In fact, both families and MLM downlines have something directly in common—it's called a genealogy!

Ever cheated on your MLM program by pursuing another one on the side? Or looked over another company's brochure and lusted in your heart?

Ever gotten overly protective of your MLM program? Trust me on this one—we have!

Ever created a lasting, fulfilling relationship with anyone while you were actively dating several others at the same time? Doubtful. Ever heard of anyone ever getting rich in MLM using the portfolio approach (several MLM programs at once)? Just as doubtful.

Think about the whole courtship ritual time line. Compare our agendas from the earliest moment of interest (in the opposite sex or an MLM opportunity) through to mature adulthood. The stereotypical, usually but not always male, junior-high-schooler was interested in "one thing." The immature, novice MLMer also seems to view his or her first MLM opportunity by not much more than how much it will "put out."

As we grew older, suddenly things like good looks and status came into play. We became at least a little more selective. We dreamed about going steady, usually with the homecoming queen or the star of the football team (or both, if we lived in California). And as we gained more experience in MLM, we too found there was more to a good MLM relationship than simple lust (in this case for money). Suddenly, previously insignificant things like the product line began to take on more significance. The company's reputation mattered (because it affected our reputation as well). We became more selective.

Then, finally, we grew up. Stability and commitment became primary considerations. Oh, attractiveness still counted, but personality and compatibility became paramount. As many of you grizzled veterans of MLM would agree, there comes a time in your MLM career when the most important question about an MLM program becomes, Will it last?

In both life and MLM, there are, of course, variations to all of this depending on whether you're a man or a woman. But even those are comparable. For example, it's said that girls mature faster than boys. How many women do you know who are promoting or operating a money-game or pyramid scheme? (In fact, the operators are almost exclusively men.) It's said that women are more attracted by

> In some ways, it's too bad that we don't treat our pursuit of and commitment to MLM opportunities even more like we do our romantic relationships.

personality and other more emotional issues. Men are more interested in physical appearance. Again, is it any wonder that men are primarily responsible for the creation and promotion of MLM programs that simply look good with little or no substance behind them?

In some ways, it's too bad that we don't treat our pursuit of and commitment to MLM opportunities even more like we do our romantic relationships.

For example, how many people do you know who married the first person they were ever attracted to? Probably zero. How many people do you know who became a distributor for, and never considered any MLM program other than, the first one they were ever introduced to? I know many (including myself) who joined the first MLM program they were ever pitched on, then discovered there was a wide wonderful world of MLM opportunities to choose from—only to realize there were others they liked a lot better.

The divorce rate in the United States is now higher than 50%. From the glass half-full point of view, that means that 50% of all married couples stay married for the rest of their lives. Can you even imagine a network marketing industry where 50% of its distributors join one company and stay committed to it for life?

Of course, one reason why some couples stay together is for the sake of the children. Have you ever stayed in an MLM program you didn't really care for anymore because you still had a downline?

Some couples with children do separate, usually followed by a bitter battle over custody. Do I even have to explain the correlation to MLM here? "Custody" battles over downlines and individual recruits are common today.

Another reason why some married couples stay together, or perhaps why those who do divorce at least attempt to work things out, is that the divorce process (at least in most states) is an expensive, time-consuming pain in the butt—even amicable, uncontested ones not involving children (trust me on this). Also, there is a guilt factor for some as well. Remember, in most marriage ceremonies, we swore to God that, for better or worse, in sickness and in health (and so on and so on) we'd stay together ". . . until death do us part."

Here's Crazy Idea #247:

What if the recruiting process involves, no, not a ceremony (unduplicatable), but at least some kind of written or verbal swearing in. Perhaps a signed (totally nonbinding, nonlegal) document in which the new recruit agrees to "marry" the opportunity, forsaking all others.

Also, make the divorce process tougher. If we had to go through some kind of elaborate, tedious, expensive process to leave an MLM opportunity to pursue another, perhaps we'd work a little harder on making our MLM marriages work.

Right now, the MLM industry seems to be mostly composed of adolescents who are being bombarded with come-ons from all directions. Is it any wonder there is so much promiscuity in this industry? Even those mature adults among us who have committed to a stable, loving relationship with an MLM opportunity are constantly being tempted by alluring competitors, and the money-game sirens have driven more than one good MLM marriage onto the rocks.

Not only are bigamy and adultery not illegal or immoral sins in network marketing—many of us openly encourage it!

(By the way, for those of you who just aren't getting it, I'm not saying MLM is full of bigamists and adulterers or that distributors practice promiscuity in the sexual sense. I'm making an analogy. MLM is full of people who fool around with more than one MLM program. Most of my readers are a pretty hip bunch and probably think I don't really need to explain this. But, trust me once again, someone is going to write me a letter or leave a voice-mail message telling me how offended he or she is being included among adulterers and bigamists—even with this paragraph.)

Yes, there are times in both marriage and MLM that it just doesn't work. Even when you did all the right things for all the right reasons. Sure, MLM divorce is as inevitable and as justified as it sometimes is in married life. Occasionally, the MLM program we're in just isn't the one we fell in love with anymore. MLM programs change just like people do. Their values change. Their appearance changes. Their personality changes. And yes, sometimes they pass away.

But still, nobody today really marries their MLM opportunity. We're all just sort of living with our MLM program. If we get mad at it, or things get a little bumpy, we just pack our bags and walk out the door. No big deal.

Perhaps it should be.

# CHAPTER THREE

# What We Should Not Be Doing (But Are)

'VE LONG BELIEVED that success or failure in network marketing is based as much, if not more, on avoiding the wrong actions as on performing the right actions. In other words, there are more people failing at this business because they are doing what they *shouldn't* be doing than because they aren't doing what they should. There are plenty of how to books on MLM that address the latter challenge, but nary a one (except, perhaps, this one) that I would classify as a "how not to" book, which would address the former, more prevalent challenge.

Possibly my biggest peeve of all, both in network marketing and life in general, involves people who don't take responsibility for their own actions (or inactions). People are always blaming someone or something else for their failures. Failed MLM distributors are a classic example. Every single thing these distributors did or didn't do that caused them to fail was a direct result of a decision that they made voluntarily, of their own free will.

Think about that. Name one situation where a failure could be completely beyond the direct control of the distributor. I bet right now there are thousands (hopefully) of readers thinking "a failed company?" What is an MLM company? It's a shipper and supplier of product and an administrator of your organization. It's essentially a service provider to *your* business. If this service provider goes out of business, find another one! Of course, keeping your organization intact can be a challenge, especially if you pick several losers in a row. Even then, it's an excuse for a setback, but not for complete failure.

Even if you lose your entire downline, there are a few million other people out there and a few hundred other companies. In fact, I know very few successful distributors who are still with their first MLM program. Most have been through several before finding a home. I've been through seven in 20 years (four in the first 3 years, but I've been committed to one for the last 5 years).

The real catalyst to this next article was an article I read in the *San Francisco Chronicle* in October 1991. The article featured a picture of two 50ish looking men with sour expressions on their faces. They were P-O'd. They were professional businessmen who had been duped into buying $5,000 worth of water purifiers. They could only sell two or three and were now forced to dump the purifiers at half their cost just to recoup some of their losses. These men were, of course, suing the company. They had been "scammed."

One of my clients in the computer business I owned at the time, who was also a personal friend, got involved with this same company about the same time. My friend wisely bought only $1,000 worth of both air and water purifiers and sold them all! My friend was not a professional businessman or salesperson, like the two men in the picture. She was a 23-year-old, junior-college student living in the Mission District of downtown San Francisco!

Staring at that picture of those two men staring back at me with those angry scowls just burned me up inside. Although the following article was written several months later, when I was in a more peaceful state of mind, I never forgot my friend and that picture.

## MLM Failures: Who's Really Responsible?

I WAS RECENTLY asked at one of my Inside Network Marketing seminars what I thought the top five reasons were for people failing in MLM. When I opened that question up to the group, I heard, again and again, stories of people who were front-end loaded, had to stockpile tons of product to meet quotas, were misled or deceived into believing in a worthless product or opportunity, were duped into believing there was little or no work involved, or simply got involved with a failed company.

Not one time during this rather lengthy exchange did anyone suggest that perhaps the individual distributor was at fault. More importantly, in no discussion in the media as to why MLM distributors fail does anyone ever put the responsibility on the *distributor*. It was always the company, or the MLM concept, that was to blame.

In no particular order, here is a list of what we've found to be the top five reasons for distributor failures. Take note, as you make your way through each point, who is *really* responsible.

## Lack of Knowledge

Many people just don't seem to take their business seriously. Heck, many won't even acknowledge it as a *business*. It's just this plaything they take out once in a while to try to get rich with. Then, of course, they toss it in the dump when it doesn't perform.

Any legitimate MLM opportunity is a serious *business*, no less genuine than any other. But they don't teach this type of free enterprise in school. No, not in Harvard, or Stanford, or anywhere else. *You* have to learn how to do it, and this education process is worthy of much more than a quick flip through your distributor manual.

If you want to make a comfortable living out of MLM, you must go to school. Read MLM books (there are many good, generic ones out there), listen to tapes, go to training meetings, read as many of the MLM publications as you can, learn everything there is to know about your product line or service, and learn about your main competitors and how to contrast and compare with them. Call up your upline and ask questions. Do your homework!

I'm not saying this has to be drudgery, or you have to be an MLM expert. But folks, it doesn't take much to be an expert in this business—compared to everyone else. With even a little expertise you'll launch yourself into the upper 5% (as far as MLM knowledge) and gain a great competitive advantage.

Aren't you joining an MLM program to be successful? A question with an almost absurdly obvious answer. Assuming you are successful, this might be the way you earn your living someday, right? If all goes as planned, this will be your livelihood for the rest of your life. People study for many years and spend tens of thousands of dollars preparing for their career. Yet, most MLMers won't spend 10 bucks for a training manual or even 10 minutes reading it!

## The Junkie Syndrome

There is no basis for this figure, but I would guess that less than 10% of all MLM distributors who have been actively pursuing this business for more than one year are still with their *first* company. Most probably have been with several. Of course, this is not always the sign of a junkie. I, personally, have been involved with several, but they kept going out of business (this was years ago, when I didn't do my homework).

I believe MLM junkies fall into two categories. First, there are those who believe, *"If I can make $1,000 doing one program, I can make $10,000 doing 10!"* These are the folks who are distributors in 10 programs simultaneously. Then there are those who believe, *"The cash is always greener on the other side of the fence."* These people are in whatever program whose tape they listened to last. They're in 10 companies in 10 months.

I know a man who used to brag about his expertise regarding the MLM industry. He was quite proud of the fact he had been involved with 21 companies over the last 15 years. Of course, he hadn't made any money in any of them, but the one he'd just signed up for was going to make him rich! Again.

MLM is like a marathon. And we all run (or maybe crawl) the 20 miles to the finish line at different speeds. And, unfortunately, there's always that guy over in the bushes, at about the 1 mile mark, whispering to you to meet him back at the starting line. He knows a shortcut that will cut 5 miles off the course! Usually, the promise is false. He just wants you to run on his course. You've lost the mile you already finished. This little scenario is then repeated over and over. Two miles in, then back to the starting line. A mile and a half in, then back to the starting line. Over and over and over. Then the disgruntled distributors stand there back at the starting line blaming their lack of progress on the track conditions, their shoes, the weather, the race officials—everyone but themselves.

Folks, everyone has, allegedly, a better deal than the one you're in. Everyone will tell you their deal will make you richer, faster, easier. Buy into that, and you'll *never* finish the race!

## Pumping Up the Volume

By this, I'm referring to artificially meeting group and personal volume quotas by stockpiling product with money out of your own pocket. This also includes the act of front-end loading your new recruits.

From all the feedback we get from the field, and from all the press MLM receives, it seems obvious that this is a major killer of MLM success, not only for the recruits who are victims of this practice, but for the experienced distributors as well. And in some cases, even the company itself is ruined by it (think laundry balls).

Several years ago, while investigating a company for a review in my newsletter, I went to an opportunity meeting and later met with one of the representatives. She strongly encouraged me to sign up for $500 worth of product since that was this program's personal *monthly* volume requirement for advancement. Of course, I *also* needed $2,000 monthly group volume, and five active front-line distributors . . . and there were five days left in the month! But that wasn't discussed. There was absolutely no excuse for her to suggest that kind of purchase, other than to increase her bonus check. By doing this she completely ruined my trust in her. And besides, front-end loading is illegal! Sure, this company didn't *require* a product purchase at start-up, but these people were actually being taught by their upline to *not* sign anyone up unless they bought at least $250 in product. Otherwise, they would "poison" their downline. I agree a new distributor *should* buy some amount of product, but at a time and amount they are comfortable with. Not by force. Which would you prefer, a distributor who does $1,000 in volume and quits in a month or two, or one who does $100 in volume for the rest of his or her life?

What I think is even worse than front-end loading, as far as cause for failure, is stockpiling. So many people out there are overanxious, lazy, desperate, or just plain ignorant when it comes to this practice. They think if they take money out of their own pocket and meet all the monthly volume quotas, they won't have to retail, or perhaps they'll sell it all later. Or they may not want to wait to naturally meet the criteria for higher bonuses by building a retail base or downline, so they buy in at some huge amount of inventory. Of course, sometimes they do this out of desperation. Their downline is dwindling fast, or maybe they had a lot of people break away all at once. This might be a fair excuse for a month or two, maybe. But I've heard of people who do this every month. There was a story going around about a guy in a popular breakaway program who purchased $3,000 worth of product every month to maintain his status level and $5,000 check, because all of his front-line people either broke away or quit. He claims to have quit this business with over $50,000 worth of product rotting in his garage. Here's a thought. Do whatever you did to develop all those front-line breakaway groups and do it again! Okay, maybe he couldn't wait. Maybe he quit his job to do this full time and couldn't afford the lower bonuses in the meantime. My suggestion: don't quit your job until your status is secured. I'm not trying to be sarcastic here, I'm simply trying to suggest that these situations all stem from bad business decisions on the part of the individual distributors.

The worst thing about this practice is that once disgruntled distributors give up and quit with this mountain of stock they've accumulated, they bad-mouth the company, their sponsors, and the industry in general. They file class action suits, go on TV, get interviewed by national magazines . . . and *every* MLM distributor suffers because of it.

### Distributor Apathy

Probably the most obvious reason for failure, in anything, is simple lack of action. Especially in MLM. So many distributors are convinced that to be successful in this industry you get *other* people to sell for you. And in many programs they even believe their upline will build their downline for them as well. And, of course, some distributors are just not very motivated or just plain lazy. They want all those wonderful benefits they heard could be achieved in MLM, but they don't want to do what is necessary to achieve them.

The more a company or its *distributors* promote their opportunities as ones that require little work or that can provide success easily, the more people they are going to attract who don't want to work, who are going to take it easy. And when they fill their downline with these people, they wonder why nothing happens.

During my seminars, I like to tell the story of a man who is looking for a chisel (an MLM opportunity), a tool he can use to carve out a sculpture (carve out a living). He does his homework. He shops around and looks over several chisels. After studying each one thoroughly, he excitedly makes the purchase (signs up). Then, he goes home and puts the chisel away. Days go by. The block of wood stands ready, but untouched. Occasionally, he takes the chisel out and ponders

**P**robably the most obvious reason for failure, in anything, is simple lack of action.

it. Fantasizes about what he could create with it. He keeps hearing great things about this brand of chisel. It's sharp, straight, and accurate. Very comfortable to hold. Once in a while, he takes a stab at it, literally. Makes a few scratches here and there. A few shavings fall to the floor. Weeks go by. The block of wood is still shapeless. Spiderwebs begin to form at its base. The man begins to notice what little effect this *chisel* has had on his carving. It's just not taking shape, he says. Damn chisel! I've been had, he thinks. My family was right all along . . . these chisels are nothing but junk! They never work. Not just this brand, but all chisels, he assumes. He throws the chisel into the trash can out back. Then, at work the next day, his coworkers ask him how his carving is doing. Terrible, he says. Those chisels are nothing but junk. Don't ever buy any of them. It's not my fault. I don't have the right tools. But I'm going to the hardware store tomor-row—I'll find *something* that works!

## I Quit!

MLM is the one form of business where you could accu-rately state, *"If you fail long enough, you will succeed."* I've heard many times that in MLM, you cannot fail, you can only quit. I believe this is almost true. Almost.

After a seminar one night a woman informed me that she was going to quit her opportunity because, after 4 months at it, she was "failing miserably." I asked her what that meant, in numbers. She replied that she had signed up only two people her first month, none the second and third, and two more her fourth month. Four in four months. She also said that those four were doing no better than her. So, they too were "failing miserably." I projected out on the white board what her downline would look like after 1 year, factoring in considerable attrition. It came out to about 20 people, which would have earned her roughly $120 per month. "See, that's horrible!" were her exact words. I asked her what she thought her downline would look like after 2 years, assuming she and every one else continued to fail just as miserably as they had the first year. Her response, with no hesitation, was "Well, 40 people." An obvious answer, right? Twenty the first year, so double it after another year. Obvious perhaps, but absolutely incorrect. I asked her to give me the number of people who were building her downline her very first day in the business. She gave the obvious and this time correct answer of "One—just me." Okay. How many people would be working to build her downline the very first day of her *second* year in the business? "Twenty, besides me" she said. Correct, since the downlines they build for themselves would also be building hers as well. So, since there are 20 times more people building her downline, wouldn't it make sense that she'd receive *twenty times* the results? If each of those 20 people "failed miserably" and all brought in only 20 people each that year, she would have 400 people in her downline—and an approximate income of $2,000 per month. Keep in mind, we assumed no heavy hitters in this scenario. Although math is perfect and the real world is not, and her actual results could vary dramatically either way, the point was clearly made.

Don't quit.

Notice where the responsibility lies within each of the preceding points. Not with the company, or its products, or its marketing plan, or even its distributor base. It falls on the distributor alone. So many distributors work the business wrong, then claim the business is wrong when it doesn't work.

Yes, the company could go under, or it could be an outright flaming scam. But if you've done your homework, the chances are increased that even this dreaded scenario could be avoided. And if it does, it will only be a setback, not an end to your MLM career.

MLM opportunities are, in one way, kind of like investing in the stock market (and I'm speaking metaphorically). If you're an aggressive participant, go for ground floor. Sure, the rewards could be greater, but be prepared to take your lumps. Conservative? Go for a stable, mature opportunity that's been around for 20 years. Or, are you somewhere in between? If you want to take the extreme risk of getting involved with a deal that's in "prelaunch," then that's *your* decision. The 95% failure rate of MLM start-ups is no secret. Pleading "lack of knowledge" of this fact is not an excuse.

What about the guy who quit his job, bought $5,000 worth of water purifiers, sold *one* to his mom, and then joined a class-action suit against the company (true story). He was deceived. Lied to. Scammed! It wasn't his fault, was it? No, not if someone held a gun to his head and forced him into it. Otherwise . . .

I hear about this kind of thing happening all the time. Some distributors make very emotional, uneducated, terrible business decisions, then look for a scapegoat. If you owned a video rental store and a supplier offered you a great deal on 1,000 copies of *Ishtar*, which you agreed to sight unseen, and later you found that only *one* was rented,

> **S**o many distributors work the business wrong, then claim the business is wrong when it doesn't work.

would you sue the supplier you bought them from? Sure, some would. But who should have read reviews, talked to critics, called other video stores, or just watched the movie first? Who's *really* responsible?

In today's information age, especially with the abundance of information sources available in the MLM industry, there is absolutely no excuse for a new distributor to go into an MLM opportunity unaware of the truth. A few simple questions, a couple of phone calls, and a little bit of reading are all someone needs to do to know exactly what will really be expected of him or her, and what to expect from MLM, to be successful.

Multilevel marketing works! The concept is sound, and the good, legitimate opportunities are everywhere. Everything you will ever need to succeed in this industry is out there, right now. The only ingredients that still need to be added to the mix are hard work, patience, knowledge, honesty, and commitment. Things *we* must provide. All of us.

We are responsible!

## Discussion

I want to expound a bit on this issue of lack of knowledge. I want to make it clear that MLM is basically a simple business to operate. Not always easy, but simple. It doesn't take a lot of business or marketing knowledge to be successful. That's one of the beauties of it.

It's not so much a lack of knowledge, per se, as a naiveté, or lack of MLM savvy. Once you have it, you gain a sophistication that allows you to see through a lot of the empty promises and hype-filled pitches that many (but not all) of the programs use to entice you.

One of the things you'll gain with your newfound MLM savvy is the realization that the actual day-to-day steps to success in this business are, as I said, actually very simple. And that bit of knowledge alone could save you hundreds or thousands of dollars in training fees! Isn't it interesting how some people will try to sponsor you by telling you how simple the business is, how it "levels the playing field," how even "Sally Homemaker and Joe Towtruck can become successful entrepreneurs," how all you have to do is "follow our turnkey, duplicatable system," then, right after you join, they start trying to sell you on the company's intensive, three-day, $900 training course? Why? I thought it was so simple!

The fact is, it is simple. The sum total of everything I know about how to build an MLM business I've recorded on three cassette tapes that I sell to my downline for $9.95. Where the real studying takes place is during your due-diligence process, when you're looking for the right opportunity. Once you've picked one, you're not on your own anymore. There should be an established track to follow.

Let's discuss another example—downline building services. Suppose you saw an ad that guaranteed this service would place at least five others in your downline within 30 days, for a fee of only $50. How can this work? Well, by making the same offer to five others, of course. How could these others refuse a deal like that? Of course, 25 more will have to accept the offer to keep those five happy. And 125 more to satisfy the guarantee to those 25. And—I'm sure you saw this coming—eventually the service will need to enroll 78,125 more who will have been guaranteed five under each of them.

Incidentally, this type of scam pops up several times a year and usually lasts about 6 or 8 months before the math blows up in the face of the perpetrator. The longest I've ever seen one last was about 30 months. It is an absolute, mathematical inevitability that a point will be reached where the promoters can't possibly honor their promise any longer. This is based on not only decades of precedent (no downline building scheme in history has ever worked) but basic logic and third-grade math. In fact, the manner in which these schemes implode is so common it has a name: the "window shade effect." Once the prefab downline has fanned out to a point where it can't get any bigger, those at the bottom stop ordering and drop out. Then those directly above stop getting a check, so they quit. Then those above them quit, and so on. So, the organization rolls down, then snaps back up, like a window shade. What's more, the poor MLM company whose program was abused in this manner (the downline building scheme must associate itself to some company's plan) eventually gets deluged with product returns. Which is why most responsible MLM companies forbid such offers by their distributors, and if one does promote such a scheme his distributorship can be terminated.

By the way, I'm using masculine pronouns here deliberately. I've never found a downline building scheme operated by a woman—not one.

A more clever way of guaranteeing a downline is the ol' reverse matrix scam. This is where a downline-building

service places about 1,000 very gullible, or at least very
trusting, individuals into usually a 2 x 9 matrix (two wide,
nine levels deep). After it fills, the perpetrator tells you,
everyone will be reentered into another 2 x 9 matrix in
reverse order! Those at the top of the first one will make
about $5,000. If you're at the bottom, don't worry. You'll be
at the top of the second and also make $5,000. If you're in
the middle, then you'll end up in the middle of both and
make $2,500 from each. Amazing! How can you lose?

Easy. The bottom level of the first matrix holds 512
people. Exactly how can 512 people be placed into the two
positions at the top of the next matrix? Remember this little mathematical rule: In any matrix that progresses $2 \times 2$,
any level will only hold two more than all previous levels
combined. So, that means that levels one through eight will
only hold 510. Not only will 256 of those bottom 512 end
up on level eight (second from the bottom) of the second
matrix, but a real unlucky two will end up on the bottom
level of both!

Or, how about this deal? All you do is pledge or promise to sign up and buy product in a company only after the
downline-building scheme has received 100 pledges after
you. Notice there is usually no guarantee that any of those
100 will actually go into your downline. And even if there
were, guess how big your organization will be once it happens? That's right. Zero. You will have one hundred people
who have promised they will join your downline as soon as
another hundred are found to place under them. And so on,
and so on. . . .

Here's a downline-building scheme (originally exposed
by Tom Schreiter in *Fortune Now*), which, quite frankly, I

think is ingenious, at least in how it makes the operator money. The offer is made to build your downline for you in exchange for, say, a $1,000 "promotional fee." This money will be used only to cover the expense of advertising, phone bills, direct mail pieces, and all the other expenses involved in building your downline for you. All you have to agree to is a minimum product purchase each month to qualify for your check. The kicker is that if after one year the promoter of the scheme has not gotten your monthly income to at least $1,000, he guarantees to refund the difference between what you are earning and your initial $1,000 fee. If you are earning nothing, you get your entire grand back. Assuming he will actually live up to his guarantee, this is another "can't lose" offer, right? Let's take a look inside.

Let's say 1,000 people go (fall) for it (not an unrealistic number, sad to say—I've seen downline-building schemes bring in 4,000 to 8,000 participants). So the operator, let's call him Sam, has $1 million in the bank. Invest that in a reasonably safe money market fund at about 5% interest and Sam's made a cool $50,000 in interest—and he's got the whole million left at the end of the year to live up to his guarantee! Not only that, but the monthly product orders those 1,000 people make each month would easily generate $50,000 in volume, earning Sam another $3,500 each month in overrides!

But wait, there's more. Many of those at the top of this thousand-person downline are going to earn commissions from the volume generated by all those below them who are ordering their monthly minimum. Let's say 200 of them average $200 in earnings per month at year's end. That's $40,000 Sam doesn't have to refund! Some distributors will not make their monthly order or will drop out, voiding the guarantee. Some will recruit and build on their own. Many who are earning $500 or more each month won't even ask for the guarantee. Sam could easily net over $150,000 free and clear after completely and promptly fulfilling his guarantee and not do one single thing to build the downline!

(Lord, why did you give me a conscience?)

Another example of a lack of MLM savvy (or "street smarts" as Robert Butwin calls it in his book) is this idea that pursuing several programs simultaneously puts you at some kind of financial advantage. Our studies have shown that 53% of all network marketers in the United States are pursuing just one MLM opportunity right now. The dual approach is being tried by 28% of them, and 11% are involved in three at the same time. So we could safely say that there is a definite lack of MLM savvy among most of the remaining 8% who are actually trying to promote four or more opportunities at once. The record, from just my own experience, for most MLM programs pursued in a lifetime is 36. Most at one time is 18! And both of these folks are still trying to find the "right" opportunity for them.

Do you know how to tell when a company is having financial troubles, or is just getting greedy? There are signals you can watch for that are a real tip-off, but are hardly ever noticed. This usually involves a cut in commissions, but some companies even manage to make the reduction appear to be a generous enhancement to the compensation plan.

For example, any time a company shifts commissions from the front-end of the plan (the early stages where most new distributors are) to the back-end (where the few highest earners are), it will create the opportunity for more income *potential* and make income projections on paper look even better—and the company's commission expense will most likely *drop!* Why? Because the company took away from the many and gave to the few. We'll discuss this concept in more detail in the compensation plan section.

I know of one fairly prominent company that added a whole new seventh level onto its plan, thus allowing another huge step of exponential growth (at least on paper). No other major change was made to the plan itself. What many excited distributors didn't notice, at least until they received their next checks, was that the basis for determining commissions was also changed from retail amounts to wholesale—and checks actually dropped as much as 30%.

Another company claims it will pay you twice, based on two different kinds of compensation plans, on the same group sales volume. One plan overlays the other. What you soon discover (usually after joining and getting your distributor kit) is that each product is assigned a point value, called bonus value, which is the basis for computing commissions—and the bonus value of each product averages about 56% of the wholesale price. Sure, you are paid on two compensation plans, but only on about half the volume!

But let's not dwell on the negative (for a change). Actually, many companies are shifting commissions the other way—from the back to the front. Some are just flat out adding more bonuses. There seems to be a trend right now toward reducing qualifications and quotas (in some cases to a fault), which will make income levels more achievable. Overall, the industry is slowly getting more and more generous!

\* \* \*

The best way to gain knowledge, to gain MLM savvy, is to ask questions: why, when, how, who. But there's kind of a catch-22 here because you already need a little MLM savvy to be able to ask the right questions.

A perfect example would be the questions we ask in our attempt to discover if an MLM program is really a pyramid scheme in disguise. It's great that so many of us are asking that question now, and I've been so pleased lately to see the diligence many new distributors are taking in their initial investigations into potential opportunities. But again, it's not so much how many questions you ask, it's *what* you ask and how you ask it that counts.

Although I am not an attorney, I've been told by those who are that if they gave life experience degrees in MLM law I could probably get one. I'm personal friends with a couple of very respected MLM attorneys and they've been gracious enough over the years to allow me to absorb every bit of information I can get out of them. There are a number of great Internet resources that provide an abundance of MLM legal information, such as mlmlaw.com and mlmatty.com. The sites for the Federal Trade Commission (ftc.gov) and the Food & Drug Administration (fda.gov) have also been very helpful in my research, as well as visits to various state attorney general sites. I've also received a great deal of valuable information via the Freedom of Information Act. For example, I requested a copy of every warning letter and courtesy letter issued by the FDA to nutritional and diet product marketers between November 1997 and January 1999. Within four weeks I had a stack of documents on my desk over 4 inches thick. It cost me $85 for printing and shipping. It was more than worth it.

The culmination of all this research went into what I hoped would be the definitive legal primer on what makes an MLM operation legally vulnerable. This article, again thanks to the Internet, is surely the most read article I've ever written.

## Pyramid, Ponzi, and Investment Schemes: Is One Hiding Behind Your MLM Program?

PYRAMID, PONZI, AND investment schemes disguised as legitimate MLM programs continue to flood the U.S. market. But unlike their predecessors, they're hiding their true nature better than ever. Many quasi-pyramids and money-games today are taking great advantage of the ignorance of most people as to what constitutes an illegal pyramid. Please understand, I do not use the term *ignorance* derogatorily. The term comes from the word *ignore*, and many of us are simply ignoring a few basic, simple facts that make up a composite of a typical pyramid or other such scheme. Also, understand that I am not an attorney, an attorney general, or a postal inspector. But I know what questions *they* ask—and so should you! Also, as I describe the legal definitions of these various kinds of schemes I'm going to use plain English. For example, where the proper legal language might refer to the payment of *consideration,* that being anything from gold dust to chickens, I'm going to assume that it's safe to just say *money*. If you want all the verbose legalese, call a lawyer.

Let's start with the ol' classic—the pyramid scheme.

By definition, a pyramid scheme is one where there is some kind of direct financial reward for the act of *recruiting* another person into the scheme. A blatant pyramid scheme would involve no product at all. You simply pay a chunk of cash to play and hope you recruit enough others to cash out, usually for several times what you originally invested.

The roots of most pyramid/MLM law is founded on the Amway versus FTC decision in 1979. Perhaps the single most defining characteristic of a legal network marketing company versus an illegal pyramid scheme came from these hearings. Essentially, the question was asked . . . "Can the last person in still make money?"

Obviously, the last person in a pyramid scheme will never make a dime. But if you were the very last person to ever sign up as a distributor for Amway, or any number of other legal MLM operations, could you still make money? Of course. By buying the product at wholesale and selling it at retail. The last person in, with no recruiting, can still make money.

If you were the last person to sign up in your MLM program, could you reasonably expect to be able to mark up the product or service and resell it to an end user, that is, someone who only wants the product or service? Are you and your downline distributors buying the products because you genuinely *want* them, or are most of the distributors making token purchases simply to satisfy a quota

in the compensation plan? Having real products of *value* to
an end user is a key element of a legal MLM enterprise.

Having said that, one of the most common and least
accurate questions you can ask in determining if something's
a pyramid scheme is simply asking, "Is there a product?"
Almost every pyramid out there today has thrown in some
kind of token product knowing you'll ask that question.
Some extremists will go so far as
to tell us that the "service" they
provide in exchange for your fee **Can the last
person in still make
money?**
is their administration of the
intake and outgo of cash. Some
will claim you are paying to
have your name added to a mailing list. Of course, the typical chain letter leads you to believe you are paying for a report
of some kind. However, there are literally dozens of schemes
out there that are not nearly as obvious. Some offer what
appears to be an abundance of bona fide, tangible products.
But again, the focus should be on *value* and *motive*.

One of the best examples I can recall was a program
called *The Ultimate Money Machine*. For $350 you were to
receive such items as luggage, a 35-mm camera, and a seminar on cassette tape valued at, of course, hundreds of dollars. Well, the camera was a cheap, plastic job that probably
had a value of less than $10, and the luggage you unrolled
from a tube. Total cost to the company for *all* of these products was probably less than $20!

A program called *Euro-Round* required a $100 payment
in exchange for nothing. Later, to "make the program
legal," they added a little book.

Schemes like Investor's International, CommonWealth, Global Prosperity, Delphin, and its various other incarnations would have you buy some literature and a few cassette tapes, with a material cost of around $10 to $20 for usually about $1,250. Their rationalization is that "information is priceless!" Okay. Let's (reluctantly) give them that. But such schemes usually withhold a larger and larger portion of your income to qualify you in subsequent stages, or cycles, and these funds are allegedly for the purchase of, usually, a live seminar on some Caribbean island. At the top stage you might end up paying as much as $100,000 for a seven-day seminar in Belize. It better be catered!

A few companies today still offer product vouchers or certificates that can be spent on items out of a catalog or from various local merchants. So, essentially they are actually only offering the *funds* to purchase these products. There is usually a commission paid once the certificate is purchased, even if it is never redeemed. The result? Nothing but paper, most of it cash, being exchanged. There is a great deal of recent legal precedent in this area. The upline should *never* be paid out of any kind of down payment, layaway, voucher purchase, or any other similar transaction that does not involve an immediate acquisition of a product or service of value. In other words, no one should get paid until an actual product gets shipped.

As to "motive," again, are you and others buying the product because you *want* that product or can *sell* that product, or are you buying it because you have to to make money? For example, if a company pays commissions on sales aids or distributor training, which several are doing as of this writing, this creates a legal vulnerability. Obviously, you can't mark up a product brochure, distributor manual, or distributor training course and resell it to someone who's not a distributor. Obviously, you would never have purchased any of these items if you weren't a distributor yourself. These are sources of income that can only be derived from recruiting because recruits are the only ones who would ever purchase them.

So don't just ask if there is a product involved. Question whether the product is even close to being worth the overall price paid. You don't have to be an economics genius to know the answer. Just ask yourself this question: "Would anyone realistically ever purchase this product or service without participating in the income opportunity?"

Thousands of people purchase products from such companies as NuSkin, Watkins, Herbalife, and Amway every day without becoming distributors. They just want the product. This is true for most of the MLM companies out there. But certainly not all.

So, now how exciting is that big ad you just saw that boasted "No selling!" Consider it a big red flag.

Now let's discuss Ponzi schemes.

First of all, a Ponzi is not the same thing as a pyramid, although Ponzis are often referred to as a pyramid. In a pyramid scheme, you pay in *X*, the pyramid promoters keep, let's say, 20% of *X* and use the other 80% to pay all those who "cash out." Not unlike legitimate MLM operations, distributors can earn far in excess of what they personally paid in, but the MLM company itself never pays out much more than 40% to 50% of every wholesale dollar that comes in.

In a Ponzi scheme, you pay $X$ to the promoter who promises that you will receive a certain specific return, say $2X$ (twice your investment) back in a few days. The promoter accomplishes this by finding another sucker who'll buy into the same promise, and he then uses the second sucker's investment to pay off the first's.

As an example, let's use Carlo Ponzi himself. Back in the early 1920s, Ponzi offered a $1,500 return on a $1,000 investment. When sucker A paid him $1,000, he then got sucker B to believe the same pitch and invest another $1,000, then took $500 from B's money to add to A's original investment, and paid A back his $1,500! Of course, a modest "service charge" was retained by Ponzi. With only $500 of B's investment still in hand, Ponzi now needed to find sucker C so he'd have another $1,000 to add to the $500 he already had, and then pay sucker B his promised $1,500. Now, he had to find yet two more suckers to have the funds to pay off sucker C. And so on, and so on.

**W**ould anyone realistically ever purchase this product or service without participating in the income opportunity?

Ponzi accumulated millions. He died a penniless ex-con.

Ask yourself this question about the program you are evaluating: "If all recruiting stopped today, would this company still be able to pay monthly commissions in the months ahead?"

Although there may be no pyramidal hierarchy involved, a Ponzi scheme does involve the need for a never-

ending flow of new participants making the initial investment. This also falls, once again, on the value of the products. If not one new person is ever again enrolled as a
distributor, could sales volume realistically continue to
move through the organization?

But there's more to consider. Let's say a company has
great products that people love and would continue to purchase even if they didn't make money. However, for every
wholesale dollar they pay to the company, the company
pays $1.05 back to the distributor force in commissions and
bonuses. In other words, their compensation plan has a
105% payout! Technically, if they really did payout more
than 100%, this would be a Ponzi scheme. The company
*must* sell one more product to cover the compensation for
the previous sale (otherwise, they'd be 5¢ short). And a
number of MLM deals today claim to have such exorbitant
payouts. In reality, they most likely do not. Probably not
even close. For example, one MLM program claims a 112%
payout, but the percentage is based on the point value of
each product (called BV, or bonus value, which is discussed
in detail later), not on the actual dollar amount—and the
BVs average about 68% of wholesale dollars. Another company promotes a 109% payout, but usually forgets to mention their 75% BV ratio, and the fact that the 60% they pay
on the first two levels (15% and 45%, respectively) is only
on the first $300 purchased by each distributor during the
month. They pay 5% on all the volume over that. Yet
another company claims a payout that actually exceeds
200%! The catch is, they pay a higher percentage on those
you personally sponsor, and the payout they display in their

ads is based on the wholly absurd scenario that every single person in your downline is personally sponsored.

So, just because someone says they payout more that they take in (over 100%) doesn't necessarily mean they are running a Ponzi scheme. There's very likely a catch. Still, considering state and federal regulators' penchant for taking a guilty-'till-proven-innocent attitude (they attack first and ask questions later), I'm curious as to why these companies would want to even create the *illusion* that they are paying out more than 100%. Why would they even want to *pretend* they are a Ponzi scheme?

> **I**f all recruiting stopped today, would this company still be able to pay monthly commissions in the months ahead?

Lastly, let's discuss "investment" schemes.

The three regulatory agencies we need to be concerned with the most, from an MLM opportunity standpoint, are the Federal Trade Commission (FTC), the Food & Drug Administration (FDA), and the often underconsidered Securities & Exchange Commission (SEC). From a personal, independent contractor standpoint, you have the IRS to worry about as well. But that's another subject. You'll likely never have to contend with either the FBI or FCC—unless, of course, that "sense of well-being" you get from your herbal product is derived from a South American poppy, or you enroll Howard Stern as a distributor.

Getting back to the SEC . . .

"Securities" are basically things you invest money in, like stocks, bonds, mutual funds, commodities, and so on.

You have to register the securities you sell with the SEC, and you have to have a license to sell them. Skip either step and you might be going away for a little while.

In 1946 (as part of the SEC versus W. J. Howey Co. decision) the Supreme Court defined an investment contract as one where "the scheme involves an investment in a common enterprise with profits to come solely from the efforts of others." (The word *scheme* is used here, and throughout this paragraph, in a basic, nonderogatory sense). So, there are three things to consider: First, is money being paid into the scheme (an investment)? Second, are a lot of other people paying money into the same scheme (a common enterprise)? Note that, so far, every MLM operation appears to meet the first two criteria. But the third test is where we depart, or *should* depart, from a security: Is the money you make from the scheme derived "solely from the efforts of others?" Well, I don't know about you, but I work my tail off about 50 hours a week building and managing my downline! Sure, your *time* investment ideally forms a bell-shaped curve (part time, then full time, then eventually back to part time), but there should always be a mandatory effort on your part to build, manage, and support your organization.

This, of course, does not bode well for schemes (I'm using the negative connotation now) where you pay a "downline building service" to build your downline for you. It appears to be undebatable that all three aspects of the "Howey test" apply to such a deal. You pay money to the same promoter that many others are, and they openly promise to do all the work for you and you simply sit back and cash the checks. Some of these scheme promoters have rationalized that they are not legally vulnerable because their service is "optional." You don't *have* to pay them to build your downline for you, you could just build it on your own, or with their help. Hmmm. So, if I have the *option* of withdrawing funds from my bank legally, that makes it okay to rob it?

In closing, I want to make it clear that this article is not necessarily based on my opinion of the way it *should* be. Much of this discussion is based on years of precedent, not just my layman's interpretation of the law. It's simply the way it is. For the record, I am a Libertarian. Personally, I believe we, as adults, should be allowed to do whatever we want with our own money as long as there is full disclosure and we are made aware of all the risks involved. The government takes (all forms of tax included) about half of our earnings, then tells us that if we don't spend the half we get to keep in the manner in which they think we should spend it, they'll take it too and put us in jail. I have a problem with that. It's *our money!* In fact, I'll go so far as to say I personally feel pyramid schemes should be legal. Not providing full disclosure about the risks and lying about the potential benefits should be against the law—and, in fact, *already are!* It's called fraud, or "deceptive trade practices." If all this information *is* provided, then we should have the right to be stupid with our own money.

Having said that, rules are rules. And until someone changes them, we've got to play by them.

My soap box is cracking. I'll step down now.

## Discussion

I'm not suggesting that any company that might be violating any of the previous three principles is necessarily going to be shut down. The only time state or federal regulators go out and search for targets is during their occasional "surf day" or "sweep day" (usually conducted by the FTC) when staff members scour the Internet looking for potential violations. Usually, however, someone must bring these companies to the attention of the regulators. As long as the scheme is keeping people happy and no one complains, and they keep their Web sites clean, it could last for years.

There are also some very good, honest programs that might not receive a positive answer to one or more of these questions. For example, I know of one very promising program that does pay commissions on sales aids. Again, that does not necessarily put the program in dire jeopardy. If a regulator has a problem with this, the program will just stop paying commissions on sales aids. Most of the time, unless it's just an outright scam, the offending company will be given the opportunity to fix the problem long before there are any serious consequences. State AGs will usually issue what's called an "intended action and opportunity to cease and desist" first before taking any legal action. This is not a "cease & desist" order. The "intended action . . . " simply means the company is being notified that the AG has a serious problem with something they're doing and is giving the company the opportunity to resolve it amicably. If the notice is not resolved or is completely ignored (which, amazingly, is sometimes the case), then the death blow is

struck. The company is sued by the state, and a cease &
desist order is served, meaning it is now a crime for that
company, or its agents and distributors, to do business in
that state.

* * *

One of the most basic concepts of MLM is to learn from
the success of your upline. Find someone who has made the
program work and duplicate what he or she did. Of course,
this same idea can be put to good use if applied in reverse.
Find people who have failed and don't do what they did.

Specific types of MLM programs have been around for
many years that simply never work. But unless you've been
around the industry for many years, you may not be aware
of this. Experience is by far the best teacher, and that's
where you'll gain most of your MLM savvy.

For those who don't have the benefit of years of MLM
exploration, here are some examples of what I mean.

## MLM Programs That Never Work—But Won't Go Away!

A PSYCHIATRIST FRIEND of mine (just a friend, I swear)
once told me that the clinical definition of insanity was the
act of doing the same thing over and over and expecting different results. For example, if you stuck your hand in the
middle of a campfire, you'd likely not do it again. If you
did, and got burned once more, you'd probably have to be
a little nuts. For sure if you tried it a third time.

So how many times do network marketers have to get
burned before we realize what's safe and what's dangerous?

In their defense, I find it rather rare that the same person subjects himself to the same doomed-to-fail type of MLM program over and over. In fact, it is usually a case of once burned and good-bye (unfortunately, it's usually good-bye to the entire industry). But think about it. If you were sitting around a campfire with five other people and each of them placed their hand in the fire and got burned, isn't it about as nuts for you to follow them? How many times do we have to watch other people get burned before we get the picture?

But that's not really fair. (I love having arguments with myself.) Most network marketers who subject themselves to doomed-to-fail MLM programs are usually new to network marketing. Let's face it. The swift turnover rate in this industry also causes it to have a very short memory.

Fine. So for all you "new" folks out there, here is a brief list of fires to not stick your hand into.

## Gold and Silver Programs

This one is number one on the list for a reason. This has to be the most doomed-to-fail type of MLM program that has ever existed. Since I've been involved with MLM I've seen dozens and dozens of gold and silver (G&S) programs start up—and go away. Over and over and over. And usually for the exact same reasons.

Over and over and over.

There are three primary reasons why these programs fail and why they will always fail:

1.  Gold is a commodity. It is an investment that increases in value. To sell it based on that premise requires a securities

license. Without one you are in violation of laws set forth by the SEC. G&S programs simply have no way of preventing their distributors from "speculating." Even if the company itself makes no promise of a future gain in value of the gold or silver, their 10,000 unlicensed, independent agents out there inevitably will.

As it is, I've rarely seen this angle avoided by even the companies. Yes, they themselves usually hype the investment value of their "product." They may not come right out and say it will be worth more in the future, but many of them do say it was worth less in the past. The SEC doesn't play semantic games like that.

This investment angle also places the entire MLM industry in jeopardy as well. There is already a fear that the SEC would like to regulate all MLM opportunities as investments. There is an ongoing push throughout the industry to separate the terms *investment* and *network marketing* as far apart as possible. G&S programs slam them both together.

2. Most G&S programs (but not all) have a system that involves the exchange of cash and commissions being paid well before a tangible product is actually received. Whether it be a voucher system, a layaway system, a down payment, or whatever, many of them allow you to submit funds and in some manner build toward the actual purchase of gold or silver coins. In the meantime though, commissions are being paid out of those funds received and a product isn't being delivered.

3. The price of gold is the price of gold. The most anyone can get it for is whatever the going rate is. This doesn't

leave much room for markup. So how do you suppose G&S programs payout 50% or more in commissions? Evidently, many federal and state regulators assume it's coming out of the next participant's initial down payment.

So number one involves securities violations, number two violates pyramid statutes, and number three would likely be classified as a Ponzi scheme.

Is it any wonder G&S programs rarely last more than 2 years?

## Discount Buyer's Services

Consumer's Buyline—gone. Mainstreet Alliance—gone. Life Plan Corporation—gone. Personal Wealth Systems—gone (absorbed actually). Success America—gone. United Buyer's Service—gone. Shopper's Advantage—gone. American Benefits Plus—gone. FundAmerica—gone. Team USA—gone. Passport to Adventure—gone.

Over and over and over.

To my knowledge, there are only three such programs currently in existence (as of this writing), all three just recently launched. Which means there are three MLM founders who didn't do their homework.

These services typically cost about $20 to administer and usually cost from $250 to as much as $795 per year when purchased through an MLM company. But the question is never really about value. After all, these services could easily save you far more than the annual fee paid. The trouble always seems to surround the fact that you could pick up comparable services from numerous other sources for a fraction of the cost, or perhaps even free! So the question keeps coming up: Are you paying $399 per year for a discount buyers service, or $39 for the service up front, then $30 per month into a pyramid scheme?

Another challenge faced by most discount buyer's services is that they simply don't pay well. Most cost between $18 and $30 per month. Even assuming a whopping 70% payout spread over about nine levels (most pay deeper), you could very well be earning less than $1.80 for every person in your downline (anything less than $3 would be considered relatively poor).

## *Prepaid Calling Cards and Long-Distance Providers*

I better start right off by saying that there are exceptions to this one. Let me qualify this. I'm only talking about prepaid calling card deals that offer *only* or *primarily* prepaid calling cards. I'm not talking about long-distance providers, voice mail or 800-number providers, or any other such telecommunications company that also happens to offer a prepaid calling card. Also, I'm only talking about LD providers that offer only or primarily long-distance service. I'm not talking about companies like American Communications Network (ACN) or Excel, both of which are successful companies that offer a variety of other products and services.

The main reason most MLM LD suppliers fail is that most are simply resellers. They are middlemen to the original carrier. With all the tremendous competition in the LD industry, the multimillion dollar advertising campaigns being waged by the "big three," and the almost absurd incentives now being offered by some companies to switch to their service, getting and keeping customers has got to be an absolute terror. Especially when those customers could bypass the reseller and get a cheaper rate directly from the original carrier.

Several months ago I was using WilTel as my long-distance carrier. I switched over to an MLM company called TeleFriend (in preparation for doing a review of the program in my newsletter) and my cost per minute shot up over 30%! When I called 700-555-4141 to verify my actual carrier—it was still WilTel! TeleFriend was simply a reseller, an extra middle man. (Note: Some, but very few, MLM long-distance providers are their own carriers.)

And besides, if you thought earning $1.80 per down-line person was bad, get this: The average residential phone bill in the United States (according to Pacific Bell) in 1994 was $34.33. In 1995 it was $25.25. Back then 15¢ a minute was a great rate. Today, 6¢ per minute is a great rate, and far more people use e-mail to communicate. So the average monthly bill has surely decreased considerably since 1995. At most 10% of that is actually paid out in commission, and that must then be spread across six or seven levels of distributors. So MLM LD services usually pay you about 35¢ to 50¢ for each customer in your downline! It takes thousands of people to add up to anything significant.

It takes about as much time, expense, and effort to recruit someone into a LD program as it does into a consumable product program. Why not pursue the one that takes a fourth as many recruits to achieve the same income?

Prepaid calling card deals usually fail because, again, they are simply buying large blocks of time from a major carrier then reselling it, but they must also build in enough margin to accommodate a 40% to 50% commission. That's why prices on these cards generally range from 30¢ to as much as 80¢ per minute. I've even seen one company offering a card at a domestic rate of $1.20 per minute! Obviously, the participants in these deals aren't choosing to pay twice to as much as six times the going rate because of the quality of the service or the pretty picture on the card. They buy them because they have to to meet the quota in the plan, and the cards are rarely marked up and resold to anyone. (See previous article.)

### Australian (Two-Up) Plans

Rather than a product or service, this is actually a type of compensation plan, a type that has literally a 100% failure rate insofar as it has never produced a "successful" MLM company. If fact, I can think of only two companies using this plan that have passed their second anniversary, and both are very minor players within the MLM industry.

Basically, in this type of plan, the commissions generated by the first two people you sign up are passed up to your sponsor. You don't start earning commissions until your third recruit, and even then you only earn the commissions generated by their first two recruits.

One major challenge to this plan is that it is conceptually mind-boggling.

The Aussie two-up is without a doubt the most perception-oriented plan. It looks fantastic on paper because it features huge numbers next to percentage signs (of course, you're only getting paid on a fraction of your downline), and it pays these bonuses downline to literal infinity (thus creating some nifty-looking income projections on paper).

But think about this: What if you signed up two people who sponsored two, who sponsored two, and so on until your downline totaled 10,000 distributors and they all were moving a total of $1 million per month in volume. Do you know what the *combined* earnings would be on all 10,000 of those distributors (including you)? That's right: A big zero!

Sure, the odds of a downline forming exactly two-by-two are totally unrealistic. But still, if there is any scenario, no matter how unlikely, where 10,000 people moving a million bucks a month in volume would not generate a single commission check—something's seriously wrong with that plan.

Australian two-ups are so unpopular that not one single company in Australia uses them!

## Discussion

Very few MLM companies today sell only or primarily long-distance service. Most, in an effort to supplement the anemic sales volume that's generated from only LD billing, have added bonuses that are derived from training packages purchased upon enrollment, usually for $195 to $495. Yes, there is certainly a legal consideration here as far as one's ability to mark up such a training package and resell it to a nondistributor. When the "can the last person in still make money" question is applied to specifically this bonus, it would seem that, clearly, the answer is no. This probably explains why most companies that employ such a bonus system try to spin them in such a way as to blur the link between the bonus and the training fee. Not all have been successful. For example, in the cases of FTC vs. Boston Finney and FTC versus FutureNet, one of the primary points of contention (among others) was the bonuses being paid from up-front training package purchases. The FTC ruled that this resulted in a direct financial reward for recruitment. In the case of California versus Destiny Telecom, the state was so adamant that Destiny never pay commissions even indirectly from marketing material or training that it included such a provision in the Consent Agreement that Destiny signed (part 5, section g), even though Destiny had never paid on any of these items in the past.

For the record, Boston Finney and Destiny Telecom have closed down; however, FutureNet has resolved its legal situation with the FTC. Part of that resolution involved discontinuing of any bonuses being paid on training package purchases.

One final comment on training bonuses: Who's your market in the United States for cookies, shampoo, and vitamins (or, what service-based MLM companies like to derogatorily refer to as "lotions and potions")? That's right. About every human being alive. What's the market size for a $495 training package on how to be an XYZ Telecom distributor? A minute fraction of 1% of the population. So it's a tough sell. What's more, these are one-time, nonconsumable purchases. The sales volume, and thus the income derived from it, occur one time for each new person who joins your downline. So, if the main source (not just one of the sources but *main* source) of your income is going to come from training bonuses, then, all legalities aside, it's just not going to be a very good opportunity as far as long-term residual income.

Those who operate discount buyers services appear to at least have sincere intentions, at least most of them. Those who attempt them genuinely seem to think they're going to do something different to break the chain of failures. They always think they've got a better way of doing it. Maybe someday someone will find it. Thomas Edison claimed he invented the light bulb by finding and eliminating every possible way it wouldn't work. If the same holds true for MLM discount buyers services, the next one should be perfect!

Gold and silver programs are a different story. Practically every one that starts up is shut down for the exact same reasons as those in the past. These operators must know going in that they'll likely be history in a year or two. But then, it doesn't take much longer than that for a million bucks to stack up in the bank. And, of course, when the ax falls they can always blame the federal or state agency that dealt the fatal blow. "Hey, it wasn't our fault," they can exclaim. "We wanted to keep paying you your commission, but those dirty government regulators made us stop." These shysters actually end up as martyrs. And, as they feign resistance to the regulatory attacks, their victims consider them heroes!

It's almost tempting, isn't it? Well, before you run out and buy that MLM company start-up manual, keep in mind that the last person who tried this maneuver was brought up on criminal charges, was found guilty on 11 counts, and is currently on the lam (in fact, he and his wife were recently featured on the television show *America's Most Wanted*).

My feeling about those who install the Aussie two-up into their MLM program is that they don't understand it. They are just as deceived by its very alluring but illusionary benefits as well. Typically, most two-up plans are changed to something else a few months after the company launches.

Some programs that use the two-up (few today) seem to acknowledge that it has some faults by overlaying other types of plans, adding various peripheral bonuses, or playing gimmicky games with it (passing up the first and third person, rotating who gets passed up, and so on). Rather than abandon an extremely flawed and discredited plan, they desperately try to fix it. Here's my favorite question again: Why?

For decades network marketers have been taught to duplicate what works—don't reinvent the wheel. Model yourself after your successful upline. Study what they are doing and just do the same thing. But, what happens when these distributors go out and start their own MLM companies? They try to design some kind of gimmick-laden compensation plan that no one's ever tried before and get into some kind of product niche no other MLM company is in!

Folks, there is a 50-year-long record of what works in this business and what doesn't. There is an Everest-size mountain of precedent to look back on—to model—to duplicate. And for 50 years, standard, consumable products have worked, and almost, but not quite (there are a handful of exceptions) everything else has failed! Look at the top 10 largest, most successful MLM operations. Nine sell tangible, consumable products (skin and hair care, nutritional products, cosmetics, home care, and so on). Primerica Services (previously A. L. Williams) might be the only exception. At least 95 of the top 100 companies sell primarily tangible, consumable products, and most of them deal mainly in diet and nutrition. Why? Because that's what works! It's what has worked for 50 years!

I think it's funny when I hear MLM companies explain that they do not offer nutritional products because so many other companies are already offering them. That makes about as much sense as the old Yogi Berra line, "Nobody ever goes to that restaurant anymore because it's always so crowded." (Or, the guy in my downline who recently told me, "Len, no one ever calls you anymore because your line's always busy"—true story.)

> **F**or decades network marketers have been taught to duplicate what works—don't reinvent the wheel. Model yourself after your successful upline.

Look back at those companies that didn't offer tangible, consumable products. NSA has been almost exclusively a water and air purification device company for years. Today, over half of their sales volume is a nutritional product. Quorum used to offer only security devices and various other electronic goods. They eventually expanded into nutritional products as well. Nikken added consumables to its line of magnetic therapeutic devices, as did The People's Network to its satellite communication network. Both Personal Wealth Systems and American Benefits Plus (which offered discount and benefits packages) added personal care and nutritional products to their lines in an effort to survive. The list goes on and on.

Nothing is truly new in this industry. Pretty much everything has been tried. Everything you see in MLM today is a variation of things that have already been done. So why don't these people just follow the same rules that we distributors have been taught to follow for half a century? Duplicate what works!

\* \* \*

A few months back, a subscriber faxed an article to me by a man who writes a column for a major San Diego newspaper. It's a business column that often deals with the issue of multilevel marketing. Needless to say, this guy is no big fan of our industry. Despite his position as a professional journalist, his writings on MLM are completely reactionary and based on little or no actual research into the subject. For example, he asserts that MLM can't possibly work because if we all signed up only six people each we'll recruit every human being on the face of the Earth in only a matter of weeks. Diehard MLM skeptics, usually those who've never been involved with an opportunity and are totally ignorant of how the business really works, actually believe this is a legitimate argument when attempting to debunk the concept of MLM. Still others, even those who are fairly well versed in the MLM biz, will tell you to stay away from the older companies because they are "saturated."

This misconception of saturation, fueled by the above-mentioned article, was the motivation for my next article.

## The Saturation Myth

HOW MANY TIMES have you been told by an unscrupulous, or perhaps just naive, MLM recruiter that the "other" program you were thinking about joining was "saturated?" Perhaps you have come to such a conclusion on your own, based simply on the number of people you know in your area doing a particular program. In fact, it is quite commonly, if not universally, accepted that your chances of success in a ground floor opportunity are better than with an old company. The logic is that new companies have few distributors, whereas old ones have thousands, even millions of distributors; therefore, there must be far fewer prospects.

Fortunately for companies like Shaklee, Amway, and Mary Kay, this assumption is, for the most part, quite false. Let us assume that 200 million Americans of working age would be considered prospects for an MLM opportunity. In other words, they are not already involved, never have been (at least seriously), and are currently employed in some type of job or business (if you don't agree with the number, use your own estimate—any really big number will work). Now, these people are your prospect base. They are your primary targets, regardless of what MLM opportunity you pursue.

Okay. So you look into Amway (the largest MLM company). Well, it has more than 1.5 million distributors just in the United States, more than any other MLM company.

Certainly Amway must have reached the saturation point. So you sign up with a new company with fewer than 1,000 distributors nationwide. Practically the whole country is virgin territory, right? Hold on.

Has that number of prospects we just discussed, be it 200 million or whatever you estimated, changed by even one single prospect? No. Regardless of which company you choose, there are still the exact same number of working Americans who have never, or at least not recently, been involved in MLM. The only thing you really gained, as far as your prospect base, are those million-and-a-half Amway distributors who you could now try to pirate away, if you so choose. Of course, you could still pirate them away from their upline into yours even if you joined Amway, so even that's not really an advantage (and it would be highly unethical).

Sure, some might say there are millions of ex-Amway distributors out there. What about them? Well, first, this number includes all distributors since the mid-1950s, not necessarily the ones out there now. Second, those who were in Amway years ago are not necessarily nonprospects now, and most of those who would no longer consider the opportunity most likely wouldn't consider any MLM again. Believe me, I've seen this many times. People who have completely given up on MLM usually blame it on the concept, not on the particular opportunity, and never on themselves.

The closest you will ever come to really having to deal with any kind of saturation problem is when a particular MLM is very hot in one localized area. But this does not defeat the myth because it would be quite naive to think that any kind of success could be achieved, in any MLM program, without your downline ever leaving your area.

I recently read an article in which a young woman was interviewed who was vehemently criticizing her MLM company for not informing her that there were a dozen other distributors in her small town of 10,000 people. She should really have been berating her sponsor, who never told her that to be successful in this business she would have to eventually go beyond her relatively small center of influence. This, by the way, involved the same opportunity that several people in other cities were calling me about— because they couldn't find a distributor in their areas to help them!

I do realize, perception is everything. And if the perception is that a particular MLM is saturated, you will have to be prepared to deal with that objection should you decide to get involved. Short of copying this article, try something like this: Ask your prospects (and you might want to try this yourself) to make their center of influence list. This list of friends, coworkers, acquaintances, and relatives usually totals more than 100 people, sometimes several hundred. Be sure your prospect does not include names of people already seriously committed to an MLM program because they would not be prospects for any other MLM at this time (or at least shouldn't be). Then ask your prospect to cross off all those on the list who would no longer be a prospect if they got involved with a "saturated" program. Usually, not one person gets crossed off.

*Discussion*

If you really think about it, saturation is rarely a bona fide objection to any particular opportunity. Would you really avoid joining a company with a million distributors because there are so few distributors left to recruit? Well, what about all those thousands of prospects who are suddenly available to you when you join that company in prelaunch?

Obviously, there is some other reason why you would-n't join that old, mature company, and why you think others wouldn't as well. Imagine your dream compensation plan—the one that you would consider to be perfect for you. What are your very favorite products that you would like your company to offer? What MLM leader do you admire the most? If any of the oldest, largest companies out there were to suddenly adopt your dream plan, add your favorite products to their line, and your favorite MLM guru wanted to personally sponsor and train you, I'll bet you'd suddenly forget all about how "saturated" they are.

\* \* \*

Who likes to listen to salespeople?

When you go shopping for a car, do you enjoy having the salesperson run over to you and follow you around the lot? What about when you are contacted by a telephone solicitor? Do you usually turn off the TV, tell the kids to be quiet, and begin to listen intently?

In fact, very few of us like to be sold anything. It involves giving up something more than our money. It involves releasing some control. It's a challenge to our free will. It makes us wonder, Did I really want that item, or was

I *sold* that item? If you know exactly what you want and you set out to obtain it, then you bought the item. No one had to sell you on the idea. It was your decision. That's different. But unless your MLM prospects come to you on their own, you will have to be one of those salespeople. You will have to find a way to sell something to them. You will have to become one of those people you usually try to avoid!

No wonder so few network marketing distributors ever actually sell anything.

Uh oh. Did I say that? How dare I break this sacred bond of secrecy by actually admitting what every MLM company already knows. The corporate videos, the opportunity meetings, the conference calls, the training manuals—they all emphasize retailing to the hilt. The impression we get is that everybody's retailing like crazy, or at least that's what we're supposed to be doing. This perception must be maintained for obvious legal reasons, and of course if a few distributors actually do sell, so much the better. And yes, there are a few exceptions where folks actually do create a retail client base. In some rare situations you will find distributors who retail thousands of dollars in product every month. I mean they actually sell it to someone else. What a concept!

The truth is, the vast majority of MLM distributors either personally consume their products, give them away as gifts and samples, or stack them up in their garage. What retailing is done usually involves intermittent sales to immediate family members or close friends and seldom requires even half of the distributor's minimum monthly product purchase from the company each month.

Understand, I am not saying this is right, or the way it should be; I'm simply telling you it's the way it is. In fact, I've gotten a good look at many genealogies in my life (far more than just my own), and I can tell you with absolute certainty that at least three-fourths of all the distributors in this business today didn't mark up and resell a single product last month.

Why? Because as a society we don't like salespeople, so we don't want to be what we don't like. Also, as a society, we can't stand rejection.

Is it any wonder that one of the most popular pitch lines for many new MLM opportunities today is "no selling required"? Many service-based companies try to convince us that because they're not selling "lotions and potions" they aren't actually selling anything (which is a complete crock). A few product-oriented companies are starting to take the "if you can't beat 'em join 'em" approach and have openly designed their programs around just personal consumption (and without incident from regulatory agencies).

Still, despite the trend away from selling, or at least using the word *sell*, it remains the one absolute in an ever-evolving more than 50-year-old-industry. Whether it's long-distance service, shampoo, water filters, or a business opportunity, something is getting sold. To claim otherwise is what I call . . .

## The Big Lie

I HATE SELLING. Loathe it. Like most people, I can't stand the rejection. I've been told I'm good at it, and it appears I am, but I would never want to make a career out of it. Knowing this of myself, it begs the question, Why did I get involved with network marketing?! Yes, about 20 years ago, something got me over this hurdle. For some reason, I got the entrepreneurial spirit and decided to get involved with a business opportunity that supposedly involved heavy retailing of products.

It appears I'm not the only one. In a study we did last year at *MarketWave*, we asked more than 600 current and ex-distributors what they disliked the most about MLM. The most common answer? Nope, not meetings. Not ethics or company failures. It wasn't stockpiling or front-end loading. It was selling! People didn't want to have to go out and sell anything. Actually, 71% of those surveyed included something to this effect among their top three answers. Amazing, isn't it?

So what would possess what must be millions of people who hate selling, or think they can't sell, to jump into a business that demands constant, effective selling skills?

The money? Sure, to some extent. But I think we should give a little credit to the American public. Most folks realize that, sure, there is the potential to make obscene wealth in MLM, but what they really expect is to earn a nice comfortable living, or just some extra spending money. And the wealth could be months or years away. Years of selling.

Actually, the answer is quite obvious. Most of these people have been convinced, at least in the beginning, that to be successful in MLM you don't have to sell anything. You get other people to sell for you!

In my early days in MLM, that is exactly what I was told. If I build this giant organization of distributors, I'll get bonuses off of all of their sales. The problem is, all those people in your downline are being told the same thing!

Today, we see all kinds of opportunities claiming "no selling necessary." They encourage distributors to just buy and consume the products themselves, or for their families. But what exactly do you call promoting your opportunity? That area of your business probably involves the most selling skills of all.

And how about selling someone on the idea that this person can be successful in the "direct selling" industry without having to sell anything?

I hear companies claim that their video or audio will "do the selling for you." Okay. How does the video convince someone to watch the video?

Or, how about this one: "It's not selling—it's sharing." Right. "Mary, I'd just love to share some of this wonderful skin cream with you—if you'll share $24.95 with me."

My all-time favorite is, "The products sell themselves." To this day, I've never seen a diet cookie jump out of a cabinet, run across the counter, pick up the phone, call up one of my friends, and start bragging about itself. Not once. (Although I can see where that would be a serious challenge for a nonvertebrate snack food without opposable thumbs—maybe that's why.)

Some programs claim no selling is required, and they'll even do all the recruiting for you. Of course, the only downlines they really build are theirs! There's just no free lunch.

Now, I realize that there are extremely "retail"-oriented companies. Yes, they encourage hard work and the heavy retailing of their products or services. The distributors, however, seem to have a different agenda. Many of them will go out of their way to make sure their prospect doesn't hear the company message. That would turn off that 71% who hate selling.

Actually, I shouldn't lump all those people who don't want to sell the products into this group. There are many distributors who feel that retailing is a mundane chore that will result in little more than a car payment. Recruiting, however, builds fortunes. So they blast their opportunity pitch at everyone in sight. They have no problem selling the sizzle. The retailing, again, they leave to their downline. They don't want to sell anything, they just want everyone else to.

This may seem as if I'm suggesting that we should all be heavily retailing even if we could personally consume to meet our quotas. Not at all. Actually, I like the personal consumption angle. I'm simply suggesting that, regardless of how the opportunity is structured, something must get sold! If not a product, then an idea, a concept, or a dream. I don't care what your product or service is, the *opportunity* is a product itself, and you can't possibly avoid selling your product to be successful—recruiting alone won't make you a penny. Or, at least it better not.

Don't be discouraged if you feel you can't sell or dislike selling. MLM can still work for you. I'm certainly one of you, and if any of the companies I was involved with during the 1980s had stayed in business, I could have been a rich man today (although it certainly has provided a wealth of knowledge). Have your upline help you. Use the tools that (hopefully) your company or upline leaders have designed to help you. Take some time to learn from those who are already successful. Build your confidence. Acquiring selling skills can come naturally, in time. Taking a comfortable, slower, more passive approach to your opportunity can delay your success—but better to succeed slowly than fail fast.

## Discussion

On that last note, let me also emphasize that the awesome power of absolutely knowing your products and opportunity are the best (at least for you) can be an incredible, life-changing experience. When you reach this point, you will be amazed at how easy it will be to sell it to others. You may even want to!

The reaction to this article was interesting in that there was very little reaction. I expected at least the retailers would object.

Writing these columns reminds me of the many years I was a baseball umpire. I always knew when I'd called a good game. As I was leaving the field no one would say a word to me. Of course, if I blew a crucial call, players and fans would always give me their overall opinion of my performance. My MLM articles work pretty much the same way. Those who believe I blew it usually don't hesitate to critique my work. If no one bothers to comment, I figure I called it right.

Suppose there'll be much reaction to this book?

* * *

I recently ran an ad in a major MLM trade publication. It cost me almost $800, but it pulled a total of 152 responses. Not bad, unless you don't count the forty-two that were not inquiries into my opportunity—they were solicitations to join theirs. Personally, I would never allow myself to be sponsored by someone who would mail opportunity pitches under the guise of a response to mine. Not only is this rather amateurish and unproductive, it's dumb. Think about it. If you had just invested $800 on a display ad promoting your opportunity, would you consider yourself a strong candidate to be leaving that opportunity anytime soon? Me neither.

In fact, downline pirates do a lot of things that just don't make any sense. These jokers are another major peeve of mine. Sometimes it's not so much what they're doing, but the brazen, even proud way in which they do it. I've encountered some who actually seem to enjoy wrecking the other person's organization more than they enjoy building their own. Fortunately, the extremists are rare and don't stick around long. But amateur pirates are everywhere, and they're real easy to spot.

I finally had my fill of these losers, and the result was this article, which I very much enjoyed writing.

> **T**he awesome power of absolutely knowing your products and opportunity are the best (at least for you) can be an incredible, life-changing experience. When you reach this point, you will be amazed at how easy it will be to sell it to others.

## Downline Pirates: The Scourge of the MLM Industry

YOUR FRIENDS ARE in a multilevel marketing program. They are dissatisfied. They jumped into the first program they ever saw and had no idea what they were really getting into. They still believe in MLM, just maybe not in this particular product or program. They're looking for something else. Knowing you are also involved in MLM, they may even ask you for a recommendation. Naturally, you tell them about your program. They like what they hear—and they join.

You are not a downline pirate!

The picture I am about to paint of these unscrupulous individuals is not going to be a pretty one. Before brush hits canvas, I wanted to make it clear that everyone who has ever pitched his MLM program to an active distributor is not necessarily a downline pirate. Your prospect could be currently involved in a blatant money-game or quasi-pyramid scheme and you only intended to show the more honest side of the industry. Perhaps you were offering a complementary program to go along with their primary program. There are a few (only a few) valid excuses for enticing current MLMers into your program.

After the painting is done, scan it carefully. Only you can judge whether you are the viewer—or the subject.

My first experience with a downline pirate came in 1979. He was the worst kind, the kind who tries to rob you from your upline into his—in the same program! I experienced decent success in that program fairly quickly and soon realized I was now choice meat. Not only did distributors from other companies covet my services, but this one guy even tried to get me to join his downline under a false name (my girlfriend's) and discreetly abandon my existing organization.

Although he had one of the largest organizations in the company (no doubt filled with shanghaied distributors from my organization), after the company folded, he was never heard from again. Ever.

About 10 years ago I came across a man in southern California who responded to a classified ad my business partner had placed for his MLM opportunity. This prospect seemed genuinely eager to receive more information and came across as very sincere. After sending him a package of information, he called my partner only to pitch him on his own program. The brochures and video my partner sent were wasted.

Already being in an investigative mode at the time, I sent this man a box filled with literature, an assortment of company brochures, many product samples, and two videos. I included a cover letter specifically requesting the return of the videos, and even included return postage. Total cost: $18.

Sure enough, he called me to tell me why his program was so much better and tried to get me to switch. During a short discussion regarding his tactics, this jerk actually told me I was out of line for being so bent out of shape, and that I should consider my $18 loss as a "cost of doing business." He went on to admit he receives "three or four" such packages a day, and that he has his office staff "trash them."

Unfortunately, the conversation didn't last long enough for me to find out if he had "trashed" the $3 for postage.

I recently came across a situation where a man described as a "real MLM pro" had been responding to generic ads placed by MLM lead generation services for the purpose of getting his name sent out to subscribers of the service. This "pro" doesn't even have to go out and find his victims—now they call him! I thought "pro" was short for professional!

Just today I talked with a woman who told me about her experience sending out a postcard promoting her program to an "MLM enthusiast" mailing list. She sent 1,000 postcards. She claimed she received 12 responses for more information, and 40 pitches on other programs!

Again and again I see information sheets that are designed specifically to recruit people from one program into another. There is always the side-by-side comparison of the comp plan, and occasionally even a comparison of products.

So who are downline pirates? Why do they do what they do? What are the repercussions?

First and foremost, a downline pirate is lazy!

I wrote an article (which appears elsewhere in this book) titled "The ABC Technique," which describes the three parts of the recruiting process. A, you must open the prospects' minds to getting involved in their own business. B, you must remove any preconceived ideas the prospect may have regarding MLM specifically. By step C, the prospect should be much more receptive to hearing about your actual opportunity. To some extent or another, you must always work through these three stages. And the first two may require the most work of all. Of course, if you prospect only those in someone else's downline, then some-one else has already done the hardest work for you!

A downline pirate is a coward!

One of the hardest parts about this business is either finding people who are interested in MLM or interesting them in it. This process may involve a lot of rejection and perhaps even ridicule. Let's face it, it's real easy to find peo-ple who are open minded about MLM—in someone else's downline.

A downline pirate is naive!

Anyone who thinks he or she can build a successful organization by loading it with people who are willing to move over as a result of a better pitch is in for a first-class education on attrition. Why do such people think they are the only downline pirates out there? Don't they realize their people are going to eventually get pitched by someone else? What do you think they're going to do the first time another "better" opportunity comes along? That's right. Poof! Downline pirates just can't seem to understand that the only people they really want from that other program are the ones they can't get!

The serious, committed people are—committed.

A downline pirate is a hypocrite!

The same clown who spent days hyping all the reasons why you should change programs will inevitably preach to you about loyalty, commitment and long-term vision—the moment someone tries to pirate you away from him.

A downline pirate is a success pirate!

Not only does stealing someone's downline reduce that person's chances for success, but you may be setting back

the pirated distributor as well. Every downline organization, if worked consistently, will eventually take on a
momentum phase much like an MLM company.
Remember, if you recruited just one person a month, and
40% a month did nothing and dropped out, and the other
60% did no better than you, you would have only about 40
people in your downline after 1 year—and more than
10,000 halfway through your fourth year.

Every time you switch to another program, you start
over on the time line. As long as you keep switching, you'll
never get to the point where geometric progression kicks in,
no matter how many you recruit personally. Downline
pirates are doing you no favors!

They aren't doing the industry any favors either. MLM
needs new blood. We must increase our numbers by attracting more professional people from outside our little world.
The timing has never been better for America to discover,
en masse, what MLM has to offer this country. One reason
why it just hasn't happened (yet) might be the way this
industry feeds on itself. We, in general, seem content to just
keep recycling the same people over and over and over, until
they drop out.

For the most part, those entering MLM for the first
time just enter the same cycle along with everybody else.
And the number of new people coming in isn't exceeding
those going out by much. Sure, we've seen the number of
MLM participants increase by five times what it was 15
years ago. But this isn't really impressive at all considering
the state of our economy over most of that time period, and
what MLM has to offer it, the immense size of the

untapped market of prospects, and good ol' geometric progression. Consider this: Over the same 15-year period, the number of people operating home-based business has increased by more than 30 times!

The reason why all these tens of millions of new home-based entrepreneurs haven't chosen MLM as their vehicle is not just skepticism—many of them just don't know about it!

Daily I come across many people who not only are not involved in MLM but are completely oblivious to it. I don't mean they don't understand it, or know of only Amway and Mary Kay, I mean they literally never heard of it! How can this be? There are 7 million people out there promoting their opportunities with the most powerful form of advertising available—the spoken word! And they've been doing it for decades. Maybe it's because so many network marketers are only speaking to each other!

> **D**ownline pirates just can't seem to understand that the only people they really want from that other program are the ones they can't get!

A downline pirate is unethical!

Some may argue that MLM distributors are free agents. They are free to take, and be offered, a better deal. It could be said that corporate headhunters "pirate" employees from other companies all the time. Why should MLM be any different? Considering that distributors are independent contractors, it should be even more acceptable, shouldn't it?

Let's not forget the differences between MLM and the corporate structure. If you quit your job to take a position with another company, the company simply replaces you. Your departure would most likely have little or no effect on your boss's income, or his boss above him, or her boss above her. In MLM, when you pirate a distributor away from another downline, you're essentially stealing money from their upline. You may very well be directly impacting their sponsor's ability to earn a livelihood and their sponsor's sponsor as well.

> **T**he timing has never been better for America to discover, en masse, what MLM has to offer this country.

Okay, sure. It may be legal. But that doesn't necessarily make it right.

A downline pirate is a lousy mentor!

This is a business of duplication. You do what successful distributors before you have done. Downline pirates who raid other people's organizations may appear to be successful recruiters to their downlines. Their downlines may even assume the role of downline pirate by example, even without the encouragement of their pirate sponsor. Pirating breeds more pirating.

A downline pirate is doomed to fail!

I've never seen a single example of a downline built through picking the fruit of other people's labor that has endured. Their "tree" may grow for a short time, but inevitably the harvester of this fallen or unripened fruit is provided sustenance for only a short time. After the fruit has gone sour or has been devoured, nothing is left. And the pirate is off to harvest more.

Successful organizations have roots. They are primarily based on seeding, nurturing, and growth. A picked long-stem rose will only last so long—a rose bush will create beauty forever if properly cared for.

Again, I must reiterate: Just because you've sent post-cards to an "MLM enthusiasts" mailing list or have advertised in an MLM trade publication that is read primarily by people already in MLM doesn't necessarily mean you are a downline pirate. Many of these people are still in the searching stage, and there will always be a high percentage of those already in MLM who are in transition—by their own accord. We're talking about the career pirate here. The jerks who feed exclusively, or at least primarily, on other people's organizations. The guy who is always looking to go one-on-one with anybody he can, to try to talk them out of their program (any way he can) and into his.

So the picture has been painted. Look at it carefully. Do you see a depiction of what is wrong with this industry? Is it an illustration of what to avoid? An image of what to not be a victim of? For some of you it may still appear to be nothing more than a white canvas, garnering no reaction at all. Still, to others, it's a self-portrait.

## Discussion

Despite the many times I tried to explain what a downline pirate was not, I still got challenges from readers who felt I had unjustly described them. The "unethical" section was the main target. These folks felt I was accusing them simply because they routinely offer their opportunity to prospects who are already involved in MLM. Not true.

Perhaps there is one other differentiation that I did not expound on quite enough. As I said, many MLMers are probably dissatisfied with their current program and wouldn't mind hearing about an alternative. Even if they're doing well and shouldn't be looking elsewhere, if they make it clear they are, then they're fair game. But pirates will hit on anybody. They'll always go for the weak and vulnerable (those who are struggling and unsure about their program), but their prey of choice are the enthusiastic go-getters, the up-and-comers. Pirates have even been known to try to latch their claws into a heavy hitter or two.

**A** picked long-stem rose will only last so long—a rose bush will create beauty forever if properly cared for.

Of course, to successfully snag those who are not looking for alternatives (like people who place $800 ads, send out $18 sample kits, or mail out 1,000 hand-labeled letters), pirates must first destroy their targets' trust and enthusiasm in their current MLM program. That's the key distinction! Pirates feel the need to create doubt, to cause you to seek out alternatives. They tear down before they build up. That makes them easy to spot. You will know you're talking to pirates if they devote a lot of time to why you should leave your current program rather than to why you should join theirs.

# CHAPTER FOUR

# The Numbers Game

I T HAS BEEN said ad nauseam that MLM is a numbers game. Probably because it is. Everything about this business is based on numbers. There are the number of prospects, number of recruits, total number of distributors in your downline, number of distributors necessary to achieve a certain stage or rank in the compensation plan, number of levels, group volume totals, personal volume requirements, commission percentages, attrition rates, company sales volume, number of years in business, number of products in the line, price of the products . . . numbers, numbers, numbers!

One of my favorite quotes, which I mentioned earlier, is "If you torture the data long enough you can make it say anything." Network marketing is an absolute chamber of horrors when it comes to the practice of number crunching. On a quiet night, if you listen real hard, you can almost hear all the pocket calculators across the country screaming out in agony. Try it on a Thursday night around 8 P.M.

213

That's when most of the MLM opportunity meetings are wrapping up.

One of my many majors in college was statistics. I was the statistician on my bowling team (I averaged 6.74 strikes per game!). When I was a kid I actually did a statistical analysis comparing the performance of Hot Wheels, Johnny Lightning, and Matchbox cars. Hot Wheels always won until it went to cheaper wheels. Today it's about even with Matchbox. Well, I'm guessing of course.

The *Baseball Encyclopedia*? I read it, cover to cover—last Tuesday night.

In 1990 and 1991 a few MLM companies were pretty much giving their distributors free rein to produce their own marketing and promotional material—and these distributors were going absolutely nuts with it. Some of the stuff that was coming across my desk back then would have made Einstein's hair stand on end (maybe he'd seen it already).

The result was a series of three articles I wrote in an attempt to enter the dungeons of MLM and free the data from its misery. My first effort was titled simply . . .

## Multilevel Marketing: The Myth Behind the Numbers

I HAVE ALWAYS been a strong advocate of multilevel marketing. I firmly believe that if it's done ethically and intelligently it can be, for most people, the only way they can ever become financially independent. How many other vehicles to wealth can you think of that involve less than $500 of start-up capital, can be pursued part-time, involve no major financial or emotional risks, and require little or no experience or special skill? The lottery and the Publishers Clearing House Sweepstakes maybe. That's it.

I preface this column with a positive note because I am not implying that this form of business is not viable and legitimate. When it comes to the numbers that are presented in many opportunity meetings and some promotional videos I have seen, however, some blatantly false assumptions are made! Or, at the very least, they lead unknowing prospects to accept certain theories that do not apply in real life.

For example, any of you involved with MLM have undoubtedly seen the "if five get five, and they get five" demonstration. It proposes that all you have to do to be successful in MLM is recruit five people who get five, who also get five, and so on. By the sixth level, they say, you'll have 19,530 people in your group (this is all based on an actual example I recently saw in a recruiting video for a major MLM company). But, of course, there is a high attrition rate in MLM (they'll humbly admit, thus giving the presentation more credibility) so we'll assume 90% of your people drop out. That will leave you with 1,953 who, let's say, all do only $100 per month, on average (mildly optimistic, but possible). Even if you are paid a "relatively low" 10% commission on your entire group's volume (actually extremely optimistic, but still possible), you will still be making $19,530 dollars a month!

Okay, so what's wrong with this picture? Well, besides the optimistic sales and commission figures, it assumes that all 19,530 people get in before even one gets out, then all 90% drop out at once! If you are going to assume a 90% dropout rate, you must assume it from the beginning. In other words, four or perhaps all five of your original first-level people are going to drop out! In reality, the average "active" percentage in most MLMs is about 25%, with 25% pursuing it on a limited basis while the other 50% dabble and drop out quickly. Please don't misunderstand. I do not question the monthly income figure, for it is quite realistic for someone working the business full time who's been doing it a while. What few people will tell you is that you may have to sponsor 25 people to find five who will go out and sponsor five others. And they'll have to do the same.

Another problem with this, or any, downline projection is that it assumes your group's hierarchy is pyramid shaped. Not only are legitimate MLM companies not pyramid schemes, their structures are not even pyramids. They're diamonds! Think about this. If your downline organization were to form a perfect pyramid you'd eventually have thousands of distributors on your bottom level and not one would have recruited a single person below them. So the "pyramid myth" is that one night you'll have 1,000 people on level five and no one on level six, and the next morning you'll suddenly have five thousand on level six. Boom, just like that. And not one single person on level six below them.

The reality is that, regardless of the size of the downline, the shaded areas shown in Figure 4.1 represent distributors who never really exist. The effect on your monthly income, using the previous example, is that you will actually only

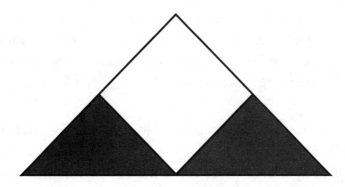

**Figure 4.1** *The mythical pyramid downlines are actually diamond-shaped.*

earn $9,765 per month with a six-level downline (if only all of us could suffer such disappointment, huh?). To achieve an actual income of $19,530 would require not 1,953 distributors (which would only account for the top half of the diamond) but possibly as much as twice that number.

This isn't all the funny stuff that goes on. Some MLM companies take advantage of this false logic and load up the highest commission rates on the bottom levels. You're supposed to think you're getting the greatest bonuses on the most number of people. Actually, the greatest number of distributors, for most people, will be somewhere in the middle levels of your organization.

There are very good, honest companies out there whose distributors still use this 5 × 5 scenario for demonstration purposes, claim they pay down infinite levels, or boast low attrition rates. Many of them are genuinely unaware of the inaccuracy of their information. I'm not suggesting you avoid those companies or distributors who use these tactics. I'm simply hoping that with this information you will be more aware of the false logic employed here, not only to present your opportunity with less risk to you and your company's credibility, but to pursue your MLM career with more realistic expectations as well.

* * *

This section isn't actually based on any single article but rather is a conglomerate of many articles and short essays (and verbal rantings) on the subject of compensation plans in general.

Let's just call it . . .

## Deep Inside MLM Compensation Plans

AS I WRITE this chapter, I must admit to feeling a bit like a magician who has turned traitor. I'm about to reveal to you how the trick works. Although I never took any MLM-compensation-plan-consultant oath of secrecy, I do feel a little like I'm selling out my profession.

Oh well.

Comp plan design is without a doubt the most perception-oriented aspect of any MLM business opportunity. There are tons of ways of making a plan appear more lucrative on paper that in reality pays no more than any other plan or perhaps even less. Every compensation plan is designed to make you rich on paper because that's the only place that new prospects can do their comparing. However . . . there's a big difference between realistic, achievable income, and potential, theoretical income.

Many companies today exploit the naiveté and igno-rance (again, meaning "to ignore") of the typical MLM prospect by creating compensation plans that have huge *percentage* payouts. They recognize that many people will assume that a plan with a total payout of 60% will make them more money than one that has a 50% payout. In fact, I know many folks who practically based their entire decision on which MLM program to join by simply adding up all the percentages in the comp plan brochure. The one with the highest total won. However, it is actually quite unusual for the higher percentage plans to really create greater incomes. Let's take, for example, plans that have total payouts of over 100%. Yes, there are several operating within the United States, as of this writing. How can they do that? Good question. (Too bad more people aren't asking.)

**There's a *big* difference between realistic, achievable income, and potential, theoretical income.**

Anytime you see a payout of more than around 60%, and surely if it's more than 70%, there *must* be one or more of the following catches: (A) Their products are grossly overpriced (compared to their cost to produce), (B) their qualifications are impossible to meet, (C) their bonus value to wholesale ratio is pathetic, (D) the founders have an entrepreneurial death wish, or (E) all of the above.

Let's analyze each point in more detail.

## Product Pricing

As discussed elsewhere in this book, there has been a massive proliferation of MLM company start-ups since the early '90s.

The resulting glut of opportunities has created a tremendous amount of competition, and most companies know that most distributors focus on comp plans (rather than the more important product volume potential). So, in an effort to offer the most lucrative compensation plan in the history of network marketing and still be able to afford it, they must increase the margin on their products. And yes, we now see some incredible payouts being offered today. We also see 5.4 ounce bottles of shampoo being sold at wholesale for $27 and run-of-the-mill vitamins offered for more than $30! No, not every company has gone this far. Some still offer reasonable prices and have kept their retail opportunity intact. Smart companies know that product volume creates income, not percentages in a comp plan—and there won't be a lot of product moving once customers pour an ounce of shampoo into their palm, lather up, then realize that's $5 worth of suds about to wash down the drain!

**S**mart companies know that product volume creates income, not percentages in a comp plan—and there won't be a lot of product moving once customers pour an ounce of shampoo into their palm, lather up, then realize that's $5 worth of suds about to wash down the drain!

When your company's computer calculates your commission check, there is a number on both sides of the multiplication sign. It's sales volume times the commission percentage that equals your income. So the equation is SV x CP = I. Or, a better way to look at it is like this: P × C = I (Products × Comp Plan = Income). Most distributors today only seem to concentrate on the C variable. How big are the percentages? What do they all add up to? How many levels deep do they go? What type of plan is it? Of course, a plan could pay 10% down 50 levels, with a total payout of a whopping 500%—and 500% of zero would be zero! The product volume part of the equation is as important, if not more so, than the compensation plan in determining the true income-generating ability of an MLM program. If enough volume flows through it, any plan will pay well. No volume and the best-looking plan in existence will fail within weeks.

## Qualifications/Quotas

The qualifications, or the quotas, in a plan also have a powerful effect on your income potential, yet they are often completely overlooked. When we do our projections on paper, or the company does them for us, we always just assume we've met all the qualifications. But, who cares how big the pot of gold is at the end of the rainbow if you can never get to it?

Some comp plans have extremely tough, challenging qualifications. There's absolutely nothing wrong or bad about being tough and challenging, as long as the degree of difficulty is fully disclosed. More challenging plans tend to offer the greatest long-term rewards. Like anything in life, the greater the value the harder we tend to work for it. Having said that, some plans are very challenging but attempt to create the illusion they are not. They try to hide the true nature of the plan. Still others have qualifications that are just plain ridiculous.

Some companies that demand very high personal or group sales volumes will rationalize that higher volume

requirements create a greater incentive to retail the products. Okay, let's admit another little MLM secret—high
group and personal volume requirements are not incentives
to retail. They are incentives to purchase wholesale! Big difference. High qualifications don't make reluctant or poor
salespeople (most of us) suddenly become great, enthusiastic salespeople. All they do is force people to buy more
inventory to satisfy a quota, so they can qualify for their
check, so they can afford to build an addition onto their
garage to hold all their inventory.

I had a discussion recently with a woman who was considering joining a company that was encouraging her to
enroll with a $4,000 product purchase so she'd immediately
qualify for the title of "Director." What was unusual about
this is that she produced corporate literature that listed reasons why she should make this large, up-front purchase.
Usually, "front-loading" is practiced by less ethical or simply
overzealous distributors and is discouraged or outrightly for-
bidden by the company itself (or, at least they feign disap-
proval). Now, understand, if someone chooses to buy
$4,000 worth of product to genuinely retail to others, with
no regard to quotas or titles, that's fine. But, even for this
legitimate reason, it still defies common sense to make such
a financial commitment to something you haven't even test-
marketed yet. However, again, the motivation to purchase
large inventories up front seems to be more to acquire a
higher rank, thus larger discounts on the product, and
higher override percentages on deeper levels. But, bigger
percentages on what? *You have no downline!* By the time you
have enough downline volume to begin taking advantage of

these higher payouts, you may achieve most or all of the $4,000 group volume qualification naturally, without having to come up with it all out of your own pocket. Sure, you might qualify for only a 10% discount on the products if you come in at the lowly "Peon" level by placing a reasonable $500 product order, and a 30% discount if you qualify for the Platinum-with-Diamonds-in-It-Master-of-the-Universe level by buying $4,000 up front. But, let's do the math on this. As a Peon, you spent $450 after the discount. As a PWDIIMOTU, you spent $2,800. So, once again, assuming you bought all this product to qualify for a higher rank, thus bigger discounts and commission percentages (not to actually mark up and resell all of it), then how, exactly, did you come out ahead financially?

A great example of how companies tend to hide the true degree of difficulty in their qualifications would be those based on "bonus volume" (BV) or some kind of point value assigned to each product, rather than on the actual purchase price. These BVs are usually an amount not much less than, or equal to, the wholesale cost of the products and in some rare cases may even be slightly higher than wholesale. There are legitimate reasons for employing a BV system, which we'll discuss in a moment. Unfortunately, BVs are ripe for abuse. In a few plans this amount is well under 70% of the distributor cost for many of the products. In other words, a plan that requires "$2,000 in group bonus volume" might actually require your group to spend as much as $3,000 or more in real dollars. Likewise, a qualification of "$200 PBV monthly" (meaning you must buy $200 in Personal Bonus Volume each month) might actually require a $250 to $300 cash outlay. What misleads unwary prospects even more is the dollar sign placed before these qualifications, when in reality they are not actual dollar figures at all. They represent product point totals. With only one exception (Amway), I have never found a company that uses BVs that will compute at least an estimate of the actual volume requirements based on real dollars.

Another example of deceptively easy qualifications would be a discussion I had recently with a man who wanted me to critique a plan that required $9,000 in accumulated group volume (over any period of time), of which at least $2,000 occurred in 1 month, to reach the level of "Executive Director" (ED). To achieve the highest pay level in the plan required him to personally recruit eight other EDs into his first level. When I asked him if he understood how hard that might be (I never implied it was impossible or unreasonable, just hard) his response was very typical. He said, "Oh, I should be able to recruit eight good people—at least!" I then asked him to estimate what percentage of all those he personally recruited would someday reach the level of Executive Director in this plan. He guessed 5%, which was reasonably optimistic (this is actually a relatively fair plan). So I said, let's be absurdly optimistic and say 10%, just to be fair. That would mean he would actually have to personally recruit *80* people, not eight, to achieve this highest stage in the comp plan. And keep in mind, I've seen plans with much tougher qualifications to reach what this plan called "Executive Director," and some demand as many as 20 of them on your first level to reach the highest paying stage.

So which sounds better: $100 per month in "bonus volume," or $200 per month in wholesale purchases? How about: 10 personally sponsored first-level directors, or 100 personally sponsored first-level distributors? It's very possible that in each of these examples the requirements are actually equal!

Again, I'm not suggesting these qualifications are unfair or unachievable. Most are, if you work hard and stay committed. It's the way they are presented that really bugs me. We play semantic games with our comp plans to make them appear more easily achievable, requiring only a little effort, then once our prospects have joined we gripe about how little effort they're putting into it. If we would all explain what's really involved with meeting certain qualifications, how much commitment and effort it really takes, maybe people would really do what it takes to meet them.

**How** a company structures its comp plan can be very telling as far as the knowledge and expertise (or lack of such) of its founders.

One final point about qualifications: How a company structures its comp plan can be very telling as far as the knowledge and expertise (or lack of such) of its founders. Two things to look for, and be wary of, are redundant or contradictory qualifiers.

A sure sign that an amateur designed the plan is when you see something like this: To achieve the title of Bronze Director you must have five personally sponsored people on your first level who each have $1,000 in monthly group volume (so, five "legs" with $1,000 in each). To earn the title of Silver Director you must have at least three Bronze Directors on your first level and $10,000 in personal group volume (meaning your entire group). But wait. If you had three Bronze Directors (with $5,000 in volume under each of them) it would be impossible to *not* have $10,000 in your own group! Unless this plan was a breakaway type of plan, this would be a redundant qualifier.

I came across a plan recently that required you to "enroll six people *ever*," of which at least two ordered $200 in product the previous month, to qualify for a matching bonus on the commissions earned of those you sponsored. The problem? This same company also requires a "one-time purchase of $200" to remain fully qualified for commissions for life. So, the qualification essentially said, "enroll six people ever, and two people each month." That's a contradictory qualifier.

### Bonus Volumes (BV)
Some companies call it "commissionable volume" (CV), some call it "point value," some call it "business volume," or any other of a number of names. Basically, as was described earlier, Bonus Volume represents a point value that is assigned to each product on which commissions and usually the qualifications are based. For example, a bottle of vitamins might have a distributor cost of $10, and a BV of 9. The percentages in the plan are applied to the BV amount, not the dollar amount. If the plan paid 10% on the level that the vitamin sale fell within, you'd be paid 10% of 9 BV, not 10% of $10, resulting in a commission of 90¢,

not $1. So, you *really* earned 9% of the actual dollar volume that falls on this level, not 10%.

Before I go any further and cause you to shun every plan that employs a BV system, let me make very clear that there are very honest and legitimate reasons for BVs. In fact, some of my favorite MLM programs use a BV system. BVs allow a company to keep their pricing within reasonable limits on products that are very expensive, and thus have a smaller profit margin for the company. For example, a bottle of shampoo might have a wholesale price of $10, as does the bottle of vitamins. However, the shampoo might cost $2 to produce and the vitamins cost $5 to produce. If the comp plan was paying a true 50% total commission, then they'd pay $5 in commission on the vitamins with no profit left for the company. So, rather than jacking up the price of the vitamins and perhaps killing the retail market for them, they instead choose to implement a BV system. The shampoo is 10 BV, and the vitamins are 6 BV. Now, they'll pay $3 in commission (50% of 6 BV) on the vitamins, leaving $2 for the company. As a distributor, the attitude you should take here is that it's better to make a portion of *something* rather than have the product be overpriced and earn all of *nothing*.

Where you see abuses is when companies use BVs to create the illusion of higher payouts. Think about this. If the BV was equal to half of the cost of every product, the plan could have a total payout of a whopping 80% (say, 10% down eight levels), but it would really be paying only a very modest 40% on the actual dollars flowing through your downline. I know of a few companies that are actually

offering payouts of over 100%, but each has BV to wholesale ratios of well under 70% (the percentages in the plan
apply to only 70¢ of each dollar). One well-known company will pay you on two different comp plans on the same
downline. One plan overlays the other, and each has about
average percentage payouts. Of course, their BVs average
about 55¢ on the dollar on most products. So, they're paying you twice, on roughly half of your volume!

Anytime you see a product price list where the majority
of products have BVs less than 80% of distributor cost, it's
likely they're trying to artificially pump up the percentages
in the comp plan. Surely if it's less than 70%. The only
other legitimate reason for BV-to-wholesale ratios of under
80% would be those few companies that resell name-brand
goods and services from other companies. Even then, there
should also be exclusive products in the line with BV-
wholesale ratios well above 80%.

Most companies are very open about their use of BVs
and clearly display them in their product price list. Some,
however, are very coy about their BVs. Prospecting literature
will only list suggested retail and distributor prices, and the
BVs aren't revealed until you buy a distributor kit. How can
you avoid this dilemma? Ask! Demand to see the BV break-
down on every product, then compute a rough average giving greater weight to what you think will be the better
moving products. This doesn't have to be an exact science.
Just get a ballpark estimate of the BV-to-wholesale ratio.

## Caps/Ceilings

Here's one more thing that can really water down a comp
plan. Although this is not very common, some plans display

very large percentages in the comp plan documentation, but those percentages are not on all of the volume. For example, one popular company claims to pay 20% and 40% on the first two levels, respectively, and well over 100% in total. Besides the fact their BVs run about 68% of product cost, they also pay the 20% and 40% on only the first $250 generated each month by each distributor on those levels. Any volume over that pays only 5%. Another company (since defunct) used to pay a healthy 10% down all seven levels, except for level three, which was 20%. In the fine print, however, I discovered that this payout only applied to the first $100 ordered each month by each distributor. Although the ordering distributor received a very generous discount on all orders over that amount, absolutely no commissions were paid upline on the extra volume. I know of a binary plan that pays 20% on the volume in the weakest leg, and another plan that pays only 10%, creating the perceptions that the first plan pays twice as much. However, the first plan pays the 20% on the volume *rounded down* to the nearest $1,000. The second plan pays 10% on *all* the volume.

**R**emember, you pay your bills with *dollars*, not *percentages*.

## Compensation Plan "Enhancements"

Every company is looking for a way to enhance its compensation plan, or at least create the illusion of an enhancement. Many companies need the profit in the beginning to cover start-up costs and keep the business stable through this most vulnerable period. But later, if all goes well, they legitimately attempt to give back to their distributors, and some have been very generous. I know some companies that have increased their payout several times with no reciprocal takeaway. Meanwhile, some companies just pool huge profits and their plans rarely ever change. One good way of knowing when your company might have a little more room to play with in their commission expense budget is when they hire $20,000 per day guest speakers for their national conventions—as several of the richest companies have done in recent years. Personally, I'd rather watch an awards ceremony where 20 hardworking distributors received $1,000 bonuses!

> **O**ne good way of knowing when your company might have a little more room to play with in their commission expense budget is when they hire $20,000 per day guest speakers for their national conventions— as several of the richest companies have done in recent years. Personally, I'd rather watch an awards ceremony where 20 hardworking distributors received $1,000 bonuses!

Naturally, every change to a comp plan is pitched as an enhancement to the field. One company, several years ago, announced on a national conference call (ironically on Halloween night) that all of its qualifications were about to almost double! And yes, this was an "enhancement" because, they rationalized, it would create an incentive to move more volume and thus create larger checks. That company eventually filed bankruptcy. Another company that was attacked for, among other things, front-loading products, was ordered by the court to change its plan so that commissions would only be paid if at least half of the product purchased by the distributors was resold to nondistributors (in other words, they *must* retail). That was also spun on a national conference call as an "enhancement." That company also filed bankruptcy.

Unfortunately, some pseudo-enhancements are not so obvious.

Let's use a hypothetical example. Let's say a comp plan is changed from . . .

| This . . . | | To this . . . | |
|------------|-----|---------------|-----|
| Level 1 | 10% | Level 1 | 5% |
| Level 2 | 10% | Level 2 | 6% |
| Level 3 | 10% | Level 3 | 10% |
| Level 4 | 10% | Level 4 | 10% |
| Level 5 | 10% | Level 5 | 10% |
| | | Level 6 | 11% |

The company not only added a full level to the payout, but its now paying out 2% more (from 50% to 52%). Virtually every distributor will perceive this to be an act of generosity on the part of the company—and the company will very likely pay *less* commission. Why? Because it removed 11% from many people and gave 99% to far fewer people.

Here's another way to create the illusion of an enhancement when it's really a take-a-way. Let's say the comp plan pays 50% total (like the previously mentioned first plan), and the BV is 90% of the distributor price. For example, a $10 bottle of vitamins is 9 BV. Then, the company raises the price of the vitamins to $11 and there is a corresponding increase in BV to 9.5. To soften the blow of the modest price increase, the company increases the payout on level one to 11% (so the total payout is now 51%). The distributors think the company just did them a favor and, in fact, it actually just *dropped* the payout by about 0.8%.

For you math geeks (like me) who want to solve the puzzle yourself, skip this paragraph. For those of you who hate math, just get to the bottom line. Here's how it works: If the company paid 50% on 9 BV, then it paid $4.50, which is actually 45% of the $10 the distributor paid for the product. By increasing the price to $11 and the BV to 9.5, the company is now paying out $4.75, which is 43.18% of the product cost. The payout dropped by 1.82%, but the company added 1% to the plan, so, voilà, a 0.82% decrease in payout. If you assumed the 25¢ increase in net pay ($4.50 to $4.75) means more income, then you're also assuming that the 10% price increase will result in a 10% increase in volume. Obviously, that's not going to happen. If you only need to do $100 per month to qualify in the comp plan, and your $100 auto-ship order now jumps up to $110, you'll likely restructure the order back down to $100, right?

The bottom line: The distributors just got a pay cut—and loved it!

## Discussion

Every compensation plan will have "breakage." This term has nothing to do with "breaking away." Breakage is the difference between the maximum potential payout and what the company actually pays. Every plan pays some amount less than the published percentages. For example, one product company I worked for claimed a total maximum pay-out of 49% but was actually paying between 22% and 26% of wholesale revenues back to the' field. I'm aware of a breakaway plan that claims a maximum of 58% that actually averages "well under 30%," according to the very honest and candid CEO. I perused the disclosures of a number of public MLM companies and found that they were actually paying anywhere from about 90% to as little as 55% of what they were claiming their plans were capable of paying out.

This is not a matter of fraud or deception, at least in most cases. It's simply a mathematical impossibility for a company to pay all commissions to everybody, all the time (although a couple of prominent companies today claim they actually are). Think about this: How much does the company payout on the product orders placed by those on the company front line? Those folks at the very top have no upline, therefore *zero* commissions are paid on their personal volume. In fact, if a plan pays, let's say, seven levels deep, then the company will pay only a portion of the total payout on the volume produced by those within the first six levels of the company. Potentially huge amounts of breakage are created by this factor alone, especially in the early stages of the company.

Again, there isn't necessarily anything wrong with this. It's just the nature of comp plan economics. Just understand that what a plan says it pays on paper will never be what the company actually pays. Of course, the closer the better.

\* \* \*

Let's take a big step backward and take a more macro view of this subject.

## The Compensation Machine

I DON'T WANT to get into much detail about specific comp plan types and their pros and cons right now. That will be the subject of my next book. (Of course, for someone who might soon become the Salman Rushdie of network marketing to already be thinking sequel—well, call me an optimist.)

In general, though, you should think of compensation plans as big machines. In one end flows product volume and out the other come your commissions and bonuses. After all, isn't that what a compensation machine is supposed to do—convert sales volume into commissions?

It seems every MLM company is doing everything it can to convince us that its machine is more efficient at this process than anyone else's. To demonstrate how powerful their compensation machines are, they paint them with pretty colors and add flashing lights, loud sirens, and all kinds of other fancy bells and whistles. They change the shape and size of the machines, add various accessories and attachments, and sometimes even connect two or three types of machines together (called "hybrid" plans). They'll give them bold, exciting names, make them customizable, and include an operations manual 3 inches thick. In fact, about the only thing they don't provide is a lifetime warranty!

All of this effort is to create the perception that their machines work better (pay more) than anyone else's machines. Do they? Probably not.

The plain and simple truth is that if you were to put the exact same amount of product volume into about three-fourths of all the compensation machines out there, just about the same amount of commissions would come out the other end. The real key is how much volume goes in, and how and to whom the commissions are distributed.

Look at the following two commission payouts. Let's assume you have the exact same number of distributors on each level for both plans. Which one do you think would actually pay more?

| Level | Plan 1 | Plan 2 |
|-------|--------|--------|
| 1     | 6%     | 5%     |
| 2     | 6%     | 5%     |
| 3     | 6%     | 5%     |
| 4     | 6%     | 5%     |
| 5     | 6%     | 5%     |
| 6     | 6%     | —      |

At first glance, most would instinctively say Plan 1 would pay more. But what if I told you that in Plan 1 you would be selling small office supplies? Things like staples, notepads, pencils, and erasers. Nothing over $2. Now in Plan 2 you would be selling high-ticket items like jewelry, water and air filters, security devices, and a line of 100 consumable, high-quality personal care and nutritional products. Now which one do you think would actually pay more?

Okay, let's assume that in both cases you are selling the exact same products for the exact same price. Now which plan would pay more? Plan 1 you say? Well, what if Plan 1 requires $10,000 in monthly group volume, $500 in monthly personal volume, and a 6-month qualification period to reach the top rank of Master Moon Rock Executive Director. To actually qualify for the 6% down all 6 levels, you need 15 other first-level, personally sponsored Master Moon Rock Executive Directors. To get the 5% down all 5 levels in Plan 2 you only have to purchase $75 worth of product each month. That's all. Sure, Plan 1 has far more income *potential*, but Plan 2 would clearly benefit far more people. The point is that there are a *lot* of other things to consider when judging the overall income potential of an MLM opportunity than just the numbers in the comp plan.

## Payout Weighting

Without getting too technical (am I too late?), payout weighting is where the bulk of the comp plan payout is focused—the "front end" (commissions and bonuses that are achieved at the earliest stages of your progression through the ranks of the plan), the middle, or the "back end" (where certain bonuses and commissions are achieved after substantial downline development has occurred).

A back-end-weighted plan would be one where the largest percentages are on the deepest levels, or the percentages are generally evenly distributed but down many generations. If there's a lot of income potential from bonus pools that are earned by only the top producing distributors, this could also indicate a heavily back-end-weighted plan.

A front-end-weighted plan is one where the bulk of the payout is on the levels closest to you. Quick start, or fast-pay bonuses, where a large one-time bonus is paid to the sponsor on the initial product order by a new recruit would also cause a shift of payout more toward the front end.

Here's an analogy. Imagine you're about to run a 20-mile marathon. However, the race promoters have been having a hard time attracting participants (it's a tough course). So, along the way, race officials are going to hand out cash to the runners who make it to certain checkpoints. They only have $10,000 in the budget for this promotion, so they have to figure out the most advantageous locations to give out the money, and how much to give out at each spot. First, they thought about placing the whole $10,000 all the way at the finish line. They expect about 1,000 runners, and historically only about 100 will make it to the finish line—so each runner who completes the race will get a $100 bill.

**P**ayout weighting is where the bulk of the comp plan payout is focused—the "front end" (commissions and bonuses that are achieved at the earliest stages of your progression through the ranks of the plan), the middle, or the "back end" (where certain bonuses and commissions are achieved after substantial downline development has occurred).

(That's like a back-end-weighted compensation plan— fewer people earn more money later in the race.) But, there was some concern that all those who thought they couldn't finish won't even bother to try. So, they thought, what if we pay each person a little less but pay more people earlier in the race? Remember, their budget only allows them to pay

$10,000 total. So, if they were to pay each runner who made it to the 10-mile mark, and they expected that about 500 runners would make it that far (it's a *very* tough course), then they could hand out $20 bills to all those who pass this point. (This would be like a middle-weighted compensation plan.) Then, one very socialistic race official suggested, Why not give the runners a cash reward at the half-mile mark—that way almost everyone would get something! Hmmm, they thought. Well, assuming just about everyone could make it that far, everyone would get a $10 bill. However, there's a $15 entry fee! Bad idea, they decide. (This would be like a very front-end-weighted plan—many people get a little bit, so it's harder for any one person to earn a lot.) Obviously, the arbitrary dollar figures I used here are not indicative of what you could earn in an MLM opportunity.

Understanding this concept and being able to recognize where the payout is weighted is absolutely critical when attempting to judge the merits of an income opportunity.

Unfortunately, many people today are being lured into extremely front- or back-heavy plans based on misconceptions. For example, when a prospect attends an opportunity meeting and listens to a guy on stage bragging about his $200,000 per month income (oh yes, it can happen), the typical prospect isn't thinking, If he can do that so can I. He's very likely thinking, If he can do that, then it should be a cinch to make just $10,000 per month! The unfortunate truth is that it's very likely going to be *harder* (certainly not impossible) to make $10,000 per month in that plan, because the few people on the stage have all the money! Well, okay, maybe not all of it, but the point here is that the

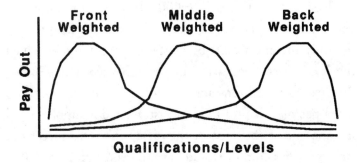

**Figure 4.2**  *Where the payout is weighted is a critical consideration when evaluating compensation plans.*

company only has so much of every dollar it can pay back to the field, and that portion isn't that much different from company to company. But, when they squeegee most of that commission to the top distributors (in other words, they shove it to the back end of the plan), it's got to come from somewhere, doesn't it? I mean, they can't just manifest money out of thin air. So, wherever they weight the compensation plan, something must get removed from other areas of the plan. That's just common sense. Imagine you have three cups in front of you, lined up one behind the other, and each one is half full (let's be optimists). If you pour water into the back cup, it *must* be removed from one of the other two cups. Likewise, if you add to the front cup then there's less water in one or both of the last two cups. An extremely front-weighted plan has just the opposite effect as a heavily back-weighted plan, but with the same end result as far as the opportunity to make a comfortable living. Now the commission base might be spread too thin. A lot more people are earning *something*, that's true, but very few are achieving $10,000 per month incomes.

I asked the more than 6,000 MLM distributors I surveyed over a 6-year period specifically what their minimum monthly income would be at the earliest point in which they'd consider themselves "successful." Amazingly, 7% said they would have been satisfied with only an extra $200 to $300 per month profit. They just wanted a supplemental income and if they got it, they'd say the were successful. Another 7% said they would have to make at least $86,000 per month (which I defined as "wealth" on the survey since that would make them a millionaire). This, of course, also demonstrated that 7% misunderstood the question on the survey. (I'll bet if they only made $25,000 per month, they'd still consider themselves successful.) The remaining 86% said they just wanted to make a "comfortable living." When I asked them to quantify that amount, it *averaged* $5,988 per month (some said $2,000, some said $20,000). The mean (most common) response was between $6,000 and $10,000 per month.

> **W**hat at least 86% of all MLM distributors are looking for, although most of them don't know it, is a middle-weighted compensation plan. The 7% who are just after "supplemental income" should be looking for a very front-heavy plan.

What this means is that what at least 86% of all MLM distributors are looking for, although most of them don't know it, is a middle-weighted compensation plan. The 7% who are just after "supplemental income" should be looking for a very front-heavy plan. Those who have to be a millionaire and nothing less will satisfy them should seek out a back-heavy plan.

## Discussion

Please keep in mind that there are going to be exceptions to practically everything discussed in this section. Trying to define MLM compensation plans is like trying to define the shape of a snowflake. If there truly are 1,200 MLM companies in operation in the United States today, then there are 1,200 different compensation machines, and no two are exactly alike.

One glaring exception relates to the alleged unfairness of plans that make a few people extremely wealthy. If you move *several billion dollars* in sales volume through *any* company's plan, no matter how it's weighted, you're going to end up with a few obscenely rich people. When applying this "obscenely rich" test to the companies you're considering, please use a little common sense and discretion.

Before we move on, there is one more thing I must get off my chest.

I once wrote an article titled "Kissing Up to the Heavy Hitters." It is, quite frankly, the worst article I've ever written. It stinks. Oh, the content was valid, as were the theories and the math behind it. But, the point I was trying to make was so utterly lost on the vast majority of those who read it, it leads me only to believe that I failed miserably in making it (fortunately, thanks to this book, I get to take another shot at it). The gist of the article was that companies needed to stop designing plans that made a few people obscenely rich while most folks lose money. I surmised that if the guy on stage making $200,000 per month were to, God forbid, have to survive on just $100,000 per month (so he must settle for one Lamborghini instead of two), that would mean that 100 people who are currently breaking even each month could be earning a $1,000 per month profit. Even better, *1,000* distributors who are currently losing $50 per month could be making a $50 per month profit, thus dramatically increasing activity and reducing attrition, thus creating even more sales volume than would have been there otherwise.

I also believe that reducing the number of distributors earning $100,000 per month, and increasing by *10 times* the number of those who earn a comfortable $10,000 per month, would only add to the credibility of the industry, not only in the eyes of the public, but also with the media and government as well. We would have, based on the above example, 10 times as many people out there proving MLM works. Obviously, the more success stories the better.

In the "Kissing Up . . ." article, I used the following comparison to demonstrate how a "share the wealth" type of plan would be fairer against a moderately back-end-heavy plan.

| Level | Plan A | | Plan B | |
|---|---|---|---|---|
| | Recruits | Payout | Recruits | Payout |
| 1 | 5 | 5% | 5 | 2% |
| 2 | 25 | 5% | 25 | 2% |
| 3 | 125 | 5% | 125 | 40% |
| 4 | 625 | 5% | 25 | |
| 5 | 125 | 6% | 5 | |
| 6 | 25 | 10% | | |
| 7 | 5 | 10% | | |
| Total | 935 | 46% | 185 | 44% |

As you can see, Plan A has 750 more people (780 more you are getting paid on), pays 2% higher commissions overall, and pays four levels deeper. Plan A beats Plan B in all three areas. Plan B can't possibly pay more, right?

Wrong. Assuming a $100 PV for both, Plan A would pay $4,950, and Plan B would pay $5,060! That's with only 185 total active distributors.

The point I was trying to make here was twofold: First, don't judge a plan based simply on how many levels it pays and what all the percentages add up to; and second, there should be more plans out there that cater to those 86% who would love to just make a nice living at this business and stop "kissing up" to the 7% who want to get rich. What I absolutely did not expect, nor was I advocating, was for companies to actually *use* anything like the exaggerated, front-heavy plan in my example. I don't believe this will work in a real-world application. I should know—it's very close to the plan I designed for one of my first consulting clients back in 1992. Hey, the theory was sure a good one. This plan did wonderful things, on paper. However, due to my own inexperience, I never considered the long-term effect or the psychology behind such a plan. It was, I'm embarrassed to say, my only comp plan design failure, and one of the most copied!

This "Kissing Up . . ." article was originally published in 1994. Since then numerous companies have popped up with plans that go even further to the extreme. They heavily weight their *second* level, sometimes paying 45% or more. From time to time I even hear that I am the inventor of these "compressed plans," I assume due to my 1992 experiment. This is a title I neither want nor deserve. In fact, compressed plans have been around since the mid-'70s, and there were at least two others in operation (that I know of) back in 1992. Every single one that has launched previous to 1996 has either added more depth to its payout or is gone. Why? Because one of two things must always happen—the company gets big, or it doesn't. One reason many such companies don't is because they can't attract leadership. Those who feel they can build large, deep downlines tend to shun plans that will only pay them primarily on the first three or four levels. When you design a plan around the concept that you are favoring the "little guy" who feels he can't build a big downline, you attract a lot of little guys who can't build big downlines! Now, if the company does grow and become successful, which has happened, then inevitably leaders with large downlines are developed. So, what do you think happens when these folks look at their commission report and realize that the vast majority of their 5,000 distributors are beyond their pay range, and if they were in a deeper paying plan they'd be making two or three times as much money? That's right. They demand the plan be changed, or they leave.

Compressed plan promoters love to show you how you'll earn $800 with just 20 people on your first two levels (you enroll four who get four more). They hype the angle that "this is a plan for the little guy . . . we don't kiss up to heavy hitters." The thing is, though, these "little guys" all have the same dream. They're the folks who made up that 86% on my survey. They can't quit their jobs and live off of $800—they want $8,000! So, why don't compressed plan advocates show you what your downline would have to look like to make the income you actually *want?* Because it would reveal that, in fact, you'd have to be a mega-recruiter to compile enough sales volume in the first few levels to achieve this kind of income. It's what I call the compressed plan paradox.

Please understand, I'm not saying compressed plans are wrong or bad. They are not. In fact, I think the intent behind them is quite noble. Again, what's wrong or bad is the way some people present them. They try to make it sound like you'll make tons more money up front but still have the same opportunity to make a comfortable living and even get rich.

Same with back-end-heavy plans. They're not better or worse, good or bad, or right or wrong, but they are sometimes presented in a misleading way. In other words, the problem isn't with the content; it's the packaging.

**A** number of good MLM programs exist today that have a balanced, middle-weighted payout. And, they come with all different types of plans (unilevel, breakaway, matrix, and binary).

A number of good MLM programs exist today that have a balanced, middle-weighted payout. And, they come with all different types of plans (unilevel, breakaway, matrix, and binary).

Just remember, a compensation plan cannot be all things to all people. You have to determine what type of plan best fits your income agenda. One size does not fit all!

* * *

Of all the MLM-related numbers we concern ourselves with, the one that we seem to care about the most is the one

imprinted on our commission check, just to the right of the
dollar sign. That's the number that measures our degree of
success in this business. What I don't understand is why
prospects seem to put so much emphasis on that number
when it belongs to someone else! We, as participants in this
industry, have been conditioned over the years to think that
what others are making in a given MLM program indicates
what we are going to make. Based on that logic, we should all
dump our downlines and start a software company (so we
can all make as much money as Bill Gates). Isn't it funny how
we would be considered foolish and irrational to base our
own personal income expectations on what the top earners in
the country are doing in any other type of business, but it's a
perfectly sensible, reasonable practice in network marketing?

Why isn't it? Well, I just happen to have written a little
essay about that. And here it is.

## How Much Money Are You Making?

I REALLY, REALLY hate this question! When I say that,
some folks immediately assume it's because I'm not making
much money. That's not it. I'm doing just fine, thank you.
I hate this question for oh so many reasons. Let us count
the ways.

To begin with, I think this should be considered just as
rude and personal a question as it is in any other form of
occupation. Imagine that question being asked of a doctor, a
lawyer, a grocery store clerk, or whom ever. Only in network
marketing is this considered an acceptable question. It's not,
folks. It's no less private an issue than in any other business.

Another reason you should not ask this question is because the answer may possibly be considered illegal. There is much precedent to show that citing specific incomes, whether in writing or verbally, or even making income projections, may be considered misleading or deceptive by various regulatory agencies unless you also state what percentage of all distributors are also earning that income, and what the average distributor is earning within your geographic area (and, perhaps, a great deal of additional disclosure). This is, of course, information few distributors possess, nor would they want to divulge.

There are also so many ways for the answer to be technically true, but not totally. If you ask for the monthly income of a prospective sponsor and he says $50,000, would that impress you? (It's okay to say yes, that would impress me too.) But, how do you know what his "net" is? What if he had to spend $50,000 to earn it? Could you duplicate that? Or, how do you know whether he moved a large downline over from another company, or purchased an existing organization, or was given one as part of a sweetheart deal (it happens)? Could you duplicate that? Or, how do you know how much of that income came from books, tapes, and other promotional material he sold to his downline? How do you know he didn't earn $75,000 the month before, and $90,000 the month before that, and $100,000 the month before that? On its own, 50k per month sounds pretty good, but placed in this perspective it now appears as if the organization is falling apart! If he made $25,000 last month and $5,000 the month before that, this would mean the company is in a phenomenal momentum stage. How do you know how the income is being distributed? What if the company paid $50,000 to 10 distributors, and thousands of others earned nothing? What if over half of all the distributors were earning at least something, and this $50,000 earner was only "average" for the company? (Both scenarios are intentionally exaggerated to emphasize the point.)

Finally, and most of all, the question has little or no bearing whatsoever on how well the compensation plan pays, how well the product moves, or how good a network marketer you are. Much like the question, "How many distributors does your company have?" your answer is more a gauge of how long you've been in business. The answer is also greatly affected by how much effort you are putting into the business and the caliber of talent in your downline. Had you asked the wealthiest, most successful network marketer in the country how much money he or she was earning the day after signing the distributor application, that person would have had to answered "nothing." Does that mean he or she is not a good network marketer or his or her compensation plan doesn't pay well? Obviously it doesn't. On the other hand, some of the wealthiest people in this business are working with compensation plans that are not at all the highest paying—but they've been working them for 10 or 20 years.

A better question might be, How much do you want to earn, and what are you going to do to earn it? How much your sponsor earns doesn't count. You can't buy groceries with your upline's money.

## Discussion

I had a prospect once who had narrowed her choices down to my opportunity and one other. The person vying for her participation in the other deal was their very highest earning distributor. He's one of these well-known MLM gurus (and this nice lady was so flattered that these two "MLM heavyweights," as she called us, were fighting over her). Well, we weren't exactly fighting, at least until he pulled out his commission check and told her to compare the size of his to mine. All stereotypical male metaphors aside, I decided to take the gloves off and go on the offensive. Normally I can dismiss this tactic when I'm going up against a new distributor who is trying to exploit his or her upline's success (with the ol' "My sponsor made . . ." routine). Many inexperienced MLMers might not yet understand the utter meaninglessness of this information. But this guy knew better, I had no doubt. He was simply exploiting the prospect's lack of experience for his own personal gain.

Here's how I handled this situation.

First, I asked her all the previous questions regarding *how* he earned his income. Or, more specifically, if *she* had asked those questions of the other guy. She said no, she hadn't even considered them.

Next, I asked her to compare the size of the two companies. Guru-guy was in a company that was postmomentum and claimed to have almost 200,000 distributors. At the time, we had about 8,000. Of course their top earner was making more than me! Not because their comp plan paid more, or their products were better, or their support system was more effective—it was simply because the other company was over 20 times larger. Again, a factor that had no bearing whatsoever on her chances for success in either company.

Finally, I asked her this hypothetical question: What if she had originally contacted my opportunity's highest earner (instead of me) and the other company's newest distributor, who had just joined that day (rather than guru-guy)? Did our products suddenly work better? Did our comp plan just improve in some way? Did *her* ability to make money just increase? Of course not. So, comparing the earnings of any two distributors from any given company makes about as much sense as comparing one randomly selected grape from two different orchards to determine which orchard you want to produce your wine from.

I've been asked by so many prospects to estimate what income they should expect after a certain amount of time. Folks, if anyone ever gives you a specific answer to that question, they're just making up a number they think sounds good to you. No one can possibly even guess at this. There are too many variables in the equation. It's like saying $X + Y + Z = 10$, then asking what the value of $X$ is. Myriad factors will determine your personal level of success, not the least of which is what *you* are going to do and how well you'll be able to do it, which your sponsor can't possibly predict. Also, how could your sponsor possibly know what those you enroll will do? I know a man who's been committed to one MLM program for over 3 years, and has personally enrolled over 60 people,

> **O**ne of network marketing's greatest benefits is that other people's efforts contribute to your success. One of network marketing's greatest challenges is that other people's efforts contribute to your success.

and not one has ever done a thing to perpetuate the downline. I enrolled a guy who has recruited maybe 4 people total. However, the very first person he enrolled brought in almost 1,000 people in 90 days. These are, of course, extreme examples. Most people's experience is somewhere in the middle. The point is, you can't possibly predict it.

One of network marketing's greatest benefits is that other people's efforts contribute to your success. One of network marketing's greatest challenges is that other people's efforts contribute to your success.

* * *

This next article is one of my all-time favorites. It was a joy to research and write. It actually was something I'd been working on for several months. As I waded through mountains of MLM material each week, I took notes of any "data torturing" I came across and put it into my "torture file." Keep in mind, most of this was just from material I'd found during the last half of 1993. And the best thing about this article is that I finally got to use the title. . . .

## If You Torture the Data Long Enough, You Can Make It Say Anything

ABOUT 20 YEARS ago, as part of an assignment for a high school civics class, I was required to attend a jury trial. I have little memory of that hearing other than it involved a medical malpractice suit—and one of the all-time classic examples of data torturing.

During that trial, there was an accusation that a monitor which measured some particular vital sign was ignored even when it began to fluctuate. The prosecution displayed a chart of the line as it appeared on the monitor, with the vertical axis to the left, and measured in increments of 0.1, 0.2, 0.3, all the way to 1.0. The line looked like a silhouette of the Himalayas. The defense attorney also brought along a chart displaying the same line, but using the same scaling of the vertical axis that appeared on the monitor itself, which was 0.5, 1.0, 1.5, 2.0, and so on. The line now displayed a couple of little ant hills.

Both attorneys presented completely factual information, based on the exact same data.

Of course, the defense attorney's earlier objection to the "adjusted" chart was sustained. The jury was instructed to disregard the first chart, but no clear explanation was given to them as to why, and they did seem confused. This amazed me, for the fallacy here seemed so obvious (of course, these were 12 people who also couldn't figure out how to get out of jury duty, so I'll give 'em a break).

Here's an example of how this same ploy is sometimes used by MLM companies. Figure 4.3 represents the annual sales of the make believe XYZ company over the 6 years it's been in business. Note the scaling of the vertical axis.

In graph A, note the slight increase in sales during the last year.

Now, look at graph B, which represents the exact same sales figures but with an altered scaling of the vertical axis. What happens?

They're suddenly in momentum! They're exploding! They're hot! Better get in now. This company is going through the roof!

Another great example of graph torturing can be found among the literature I've received for an MLM vitamin company. Figure 4.4 is an approximation of a graph the

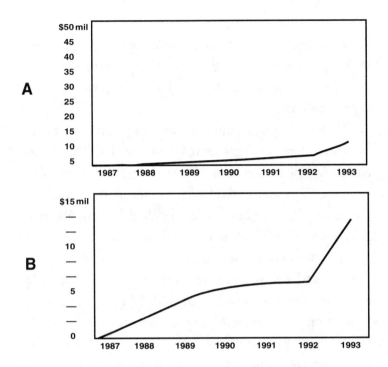

**Figure 4.3**   *This is a prime example of graph manipulation.*

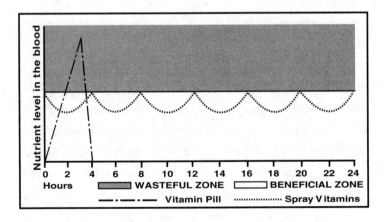

**Figure 4.4**   *Another example of graph manipulation.*

company has presented that shows the nutrient level within the bloodstream when vitamin tablets are used, compared with its vitamin spray. (Because this is a rather litigious company, I'm not using the actual graph, but rather a close approximation.)

Notice, the graph compares one dose of vitamin tablets to several doses of spray throughout the day. This is like comparing the hunger levels of someone who ate once in the morning to someone who had three full meals. And notice the curious upswings in nutrient levels that occur about an hour *before* each dose of spray. Exactly how does that happen?

Another example was a graph recently published in a popular national magazine that accompanied an article by a top distributor for a well-known MLM company. He was comparing the virtues of the breakaway plan with the matrix plan. To demonstrate the advantages of the breakaway plan, he displayed a graph showing the number of people who would fall on each level in a 3 × 4 matrix (three wide, four level deep) compared with that of an unlimited width breakaway plan. Not only did he choose an extremely weak form of matrix that doesn't exist anywhere in the industry, but he also compared the numbers it would generate to his actual downline! Keep in mind, a 3 × 4 matrix would only accommodate 120 people, and the author's actual organization exceeds 35,000 thousand people! Making this comparison is like saying Chevrolets are faster than Fords by comparing a Corvette with a Pinto, or that the American League is better than the National League by comparing the 1927 Yankees to the 1962 Mets.

Graph fudging isn't always used to promote; it's sometimes used to detract. For example, when *Forbes* magazine attacked Herbalife some months back, the magazine displayed graphs showing how sales figures in four foreign countries had risen, then fallen. Of course, no graph was included that showed that U.S. sales had risen, then fallen—then risen again! Also, Herbalife is in 15 countries, and it seems as if only those where this severe drop occurred were chosen to be represented in this graph. What about the other 11 countries?

This practice of companies only picking targets that serve them is also widespread. Some years ago, a now defunct MLM company was comparing the price of its laundry detergent with that of three other name brands. It beat the price of all three, giving the impression it offered the best price. What I discovered was that there were 13 brands available at my local supermarket, and those 3 name brands were, in fact, higher in price—and the other 10 were lower! The MLM product was actually the fourth most expensive.

**A** thousand new recruits a month is great—unless 1,500 are leaving.

Then there's the mysterious crystal ball graph. These have "projected" sales for the following year with a line that goes practically straight up at the end. It seems practically every MLM company is going to go into a massive momentum phase next year.

I also can't stand to read about a 3-month-old company claiming to have monthly sales increases of 3000%. Think about that. It could have sold $100 the first month and $4,000 the third, which would be a "3000% increase" but still pitiful overall sales. The percentage of increase means very little. It's how much it sold that counts.

Many companies claim that so many thousands of new distributors are signing up each month. Notice, they never tell you how many are dropping out. A thousand new recruits a month is great—unless 1,500 are leaving.

I've been hearing a lot lately about companies that claim to have signed up, say, 1,000 people their first month, and now have 2,000 after 4 months (an "average monthly increase of 33%!"). The implication is that they're still growing strong. Are they? Could be. Or, they signed up 1,000 their first month, 700 the second, 300 the third, and not one solitary distributor application was received during the fourth month.

Here's an interesting case, based on an actual situation, where a company was claiming to have "doubled in size in the last 2 years" but competitors were claiming they had lost a third of their sales base—and both sides were right! How? Well, the first year they did about 10 million in sales, then 30 million the second year, then 20 million the third. Did their sales drop by 33%, or did they increase by 100%? The answer: Yes.

And what about this newest myth going around that the Direct Selling Association (DSA) claims that the average MLM distributor recruits 2.7 people? (The DSA never cited such a figure.) For years the figure was 2.6, allegedly taken from some research a top Nu kin distributor had conducted several years ago. Our survey of more than 6,000 MLMers over the last 6 years came up with 2.1.

Guess what? We're all wrong. It's mathematically impossible for this number to be greater than one. Really think about this stuff. If every distributor who ever joined an MLM opportunity over the last 50 years recruited an average of even two others, we would, in fact, have recruited every man, woman, child, statue, mannequin, snowman, and crash dummy on the face of the earth. We'd be going beyond the Earth. We would be the ones landing on alien planets saying, "Take us to your upline group leader!"

Income data can be torturing as well. For example, one major MLM company claims to have created more women millionaires than any other company in America. The top earner in that company earns about $500,000 per year, however. The company is referring to *lifetime* earnings. Based on that definition, then just about all of us are going to be millionaires someday!

I know a guy who has publicly stated he's had "over 70,000 people in my organization." Actually, he's never had more than 6,000 at one time. He's referring to all the distributors he's ever had in all the companies he's ever been in, which sounds a lot better, doesn't it?

I'm certainly not suggesting that every statistical claim made in this industry is bogus or misleading. In fact, most are not. But we as a group, meaning us MLMers, really need to stop taking everything on faith. Think about what you are told. Question it. Even suspect it.

When your and your family's personal and financial well-being are at stake, there's nothing wrong with assuming a little guilt until innocence is proven.

## Discussion

One currently hot MLM company (as of this writing) claims it has amassed 300,000 distributors in the first four years. Another is claiming 87,000 in the first 18 months. What they're not telling anyone (unless you ask, as I did) is that they have yet to purge their database of inactive or retired distributors. They don't currently have 300,000 or 87,000 distributors. What they have are that many total distributor applications—including those of people who quit months or years ago. One has no enrollment fee to be a distributor and absolutely absurd retail pricing. So thousands of those being counted as "distributors" are really just wholesale customers who sign up just to get the product cheaper. This same company is also claiming monthly sales of $8.5 million, but that's based on its ridiculous 100% suggested retail markup. Therefore, sales are actually $4.25 million.

Several companies use what is called a "binary" compensation plan. In general, I don't really care for binaries, although this type of plan does offer some unique and powerful benefits. But one alleged advantage it really does not have is that it pays "infinitely" in depth. After some mathematical analysis, I discovered that the commission portion of any particular sale was approximately halved each level upline. In other words, if the company wanted to pay $50 in commissions to the field on a $100 purchase, $25 would be paid to the first level upline from the sale, then $12.50 to the next qualified person above him or her, then $6.25, then $3.13, and so on up the line—theoretically forever! Why? Because any number in the universe, no matter how small it gets, can still be divided by

> I've found that a shift is occurring in the diligence levels and expectations of most *new* MLM prospects. For them, hype is out, and truth is in.

two, correct? So does it really pay infinitely? Yes, if you don't mind earning .00005¢ on a $100 sale on your 20th level.

I guess the previous article was an example of torturing the data until it tells the truth!

* * *

Being a distributor myself, I'm often asked various statistical questions about my opportunity. Although most are fair and valid questions, I used to hate having to answer them (though I always did). The reason is that in this business, you sometimes (not always) place yourself at a marketing disadvantage by telling the truth. Call me a cynic (and oh, if I only had a dollar for every time someone has), but I'm always concerned that my truths may not be as good as the other guy's hype and exaggerations.

Over the last couple of years or so, I've found that a shift is occurring in the diligence levels and expectations of most *new* MLM prospects. For them, hype is out, and truth is in. Those outer circle folks looking at MLM for the first time seem to have become a pretty jaded, more professional group overall. More and more of them are following the "opportunity seeker's" golden rule: If it sounds too good to be true, it probably is. To these folks, at least the serious ones, it's become a lot easier to sound "too good."

Unfortunately, the industry seems to be lagging in this realization. Although the prospect base demands truth and accuracy, the majority of MLM companies and distributors (but certainly not all) still seem bent on torturing the data to their advantage.

Here's an article that deals specifically with one particular very tortured statistic—recruiting figures.

# How to Recruit 100 Distributors a Day, Every Day of the Week!

I WAS EXPLORING the Internet jungle a few weeks ago when I stumbled on what appeared to be an open MLM forum. It had pretty much been taken over by distributors for one dominant opportunity, however. Dare any member from a subordinate MLM species wander into their domain and there would be a frenzy of activity to see who could convince the newcomer that their MLM program was superior—and from the looks of their online conversations, they were succeeding.

The lure wasn't the promise of quick and easy wealth, for there was actually little mention of high incomes. Nor was it the miraculous benefits of their amazing product line. Instead, they were trading recruiting figures. Massive recruiting figures.

One had recruited 11 people his first day in the business. Another claimed she built a downline of more than 3,500 by her second month. Yet another claimed the company as a whole had gained more than 180,000 distributors since January. And yes, one even claimed he had "personally recruited 100 people in a single day!"

This would all be very impressive—if I could buy groceries with distributor applications.

It's fascinating how the marketing trends in this industry evolve from year to year. In 1991 and 1992 everyone bragged about how much their top earners were making. In 1993 and 1994 everyone was hyping their company's total monthly sales or sales growth. And in the middle of this time span I remember a short-lived phase in which the age of a company seemed most important. From about 1995 through 1997 everyone was talking about how many distributors his or her company had. It was a phase where what is actually one of the least important factors was considered the most important. Today the big selling point is, alas, how little effort you must apply. The recruiting system that can allegedly generate the largest downline with the least amount of work is king. But, to demonstrate that system's effectiveness, recruiting numbers are still paramount.

So, to create a marketing advantage, the in thing now seems to be how to redefine "distributor" to claim the highest possible number of them. For example, many companies have recently gone into make-believe momentum by having a free sign-up system via an 800 number (in fact, in some of these programs, you can even sign up distributors without them knowing it). So, retail customers now routinely sign up as "distributors" to get the product at wholesale.

Several companies now allow their distributors to sign up their spouse, or any family members, and some even allow you to sign yourself up as many times as you want! Others technically forbid such practices, but their distributors are doing it anyway and without consequence. So although the company may only gain 200 actual distributors next month, it may be able to claim an increase of more than 1,000 distributorships.

The technique is to simply give out sequential ID numbers to anyone who orders even a single product, one time, and to all the positions occupied by each distributor. Then, call each ID number a "distributor."

Another way to make sure that this number always increases is to never purge your inactive distributors.

Technically, a company can't terminate a person for not ordering product. (Although MLM companies, like any direct sales company, can require a sales quota to earn commissions, they can't require a product purchase just to maintain distributor status.) Instead, most will place nonordering distributors in an "inactive" file and simply remove them from the distributor hierarchy. Some, however, will continue to count these people in their total distributor figure because they are, technically, still distributors.

Most MLM companies have some sort of annual renewal process in which a small administration fee is charged, or at least they have a reapplication process to weed out the dead wood. Of course, if you omit this process, and inactive distributors are still technically considered in the program, then essentially they are "distributors" for life! No matter how many quit, the "total distributor" figure will always climb. What's more, the company can now claim a "zero percent attrition rate!"

And it would be true—technically.

MLM programs that employ a binary compensation plan have a unique advantage in this area that's exclusively their own. In a binary, one person can potentially occupy numerous "income centers." I know of at least two such companies that are currently claiming a "total distributor" figure based on the total number of income centers. Fortunately, most of the binary plan contingent have not followed suit.

So here's the formula to build a "1-million distributor company" within 5 years:

1. Allow anyone to sign up for free, over the phone.
2. Count product customers as distributors, even if they only order once and you never hear from them again.
3. Allow them to sign up as many times as they want, or disallow it but look the other way.
4. Allow them to sign up all family members.
5. Never purge your company database of inactive distributors.

(Or, you can just not reveal your total distributor figure and let your distributors "estimate." That should at least triple the actual amount.)

Just imagine if Amway or Shaklee adopted the previous criteria when defining "distributor." They could easily claim to have 100 million of them by now! I recently saw an ad for a popular MLM program with the headline "Over 300,000 people have joined (blank) International!" Of course, the ad doesn't mention that about 225,000 are no longer active. Another company recently claimed to have 156,000 distributors but really had just over 60,000 who were still ordering product. Yet another popular company was claiming to have over 700,000 reps yet cut only 16,000 distributor checks that month.

So, let's get to the big question: How can you, personally, recruit 100 distributors a day, every day of the week? Simple. Get your company to employ the following recruiting system: You walk up to someone on the street, tap him or her on the shoulder twice with the index finger of your right hand, and say "I dub thee a distributor." That's it!

Think about the possibilities. You could literally recruit 1,000 new distributors each day if you found a busy intersection in a major city. And if you trained just a handful of people in your downline to do the same, you could build an organization larger than 10,000 within days! And, of course, your company could easily claim to have more than one million distributors within just a few short weeks.

Now, understand, no one will make one thin dime in commissions. But remember, easy systems and big recruiting numbers count . . . right?

\* \* \*

In all modesty, I believe that *MarketWave* is the only company that has ever done a long-term statistical analysis of network marketing. I don't mean a quick survey here and there, but an ongoing, ever-increasing storehouse of MLM data. Unfortunately, most statistical data isn't worth a hill o' bean counters unless you have a quantity of it. For example, Ty Cobb holds the Major League record for highest career batting average at .367, despite the fact that an outfielder for the Cleveland Indians by the name of Jackie Gallagher had a "one-thousand" career batting average! Of course, 'ol Jackie only got to bat once and got one hit.

I recruited four of the first six people I ever prospected. Do you think I maintained that 67% recruiting ratio? No, it dropped a little after the next 22 straight prospects said "no."

So despite an ongoing effort to put the numbers together over the last 10 years (beginning in late 1990), it was not until about January 1994 that I really had sufficient numbers to say anything valid about the industry. Today, these numbers provide solid information.

This information was derived from many sources, including formal surveys (passed out at all my Inside Network Marketing seminars around the country and published at least once a year in the *MarketWave Alert Letter*), short mini-surveys found on the back of subscription renewal coupons, personal interviews, my personal database of more than 33,000 MLMers who have contacted me since October 1990, and approximately 1,400 pages of notes from all my telephone conversations over the last 10 years.

This information was updated July 30, 1999.

## Survey Results (And What They Mean)

**Average age of distributor: 37.8 years.** And rising! Professionals, white-collar workers, vulnerable middle managers, and retired folks are discovering MLM. To put this in perspective, the average American is just over 35 years old.

**Sex: Male, 52%; Female, 39%; Business/Trust, 4%; Couples, 5%.** The result of this question continues to amaze me, and it is probably the most challenged, but the data shows this is *not* a business primarily pursued by women, at least not any more. What's more, the number of men is rising, perhaps because more of them fall into the categories listed in the preceding section. Another explanation for this statistical enigma might be that the female-oriented home-party type MLMs are now much rarer than they were in the '60s and '70s, and the largest of those that still exist, such as Tupperware, Avon, and Mary Kay, generally don't run with the typical "MLM" crowd and therefore would be far less

likely to respond to an MLM survey. Also, many husband-
and-wife teams are registered only under the man's name
(however politically incorrect this may be). I'd guess that if
you were to drop the number of men by 10% and increase
"couples" by the same amount, you might get a more accurate picture.

**Primary reason for joining an MLM program:**

| Reason | Men | Women | All |
|---|---|---|---|
| More money | 62% | 41% | 52% |
| More free time | 26% | 34% | 31% |
| Purchase products | 5% | 15% | 9% |
| Other | 7% | 10% | 8% |

Actually, most responses did usually fall within these
three general categories. "More money" responses included
those that involved any material gain, such as "new house"
or "retirement account." "More free time" responses
included such goals as "waking up later," "spending more
time with family," or "work at home/no commuting."
"Other" usually involved personal goals such as "personal
development," "self-esteem," or "meet more people."

By the way, the majority of those who answered with
just "more money" who were asked why they wanted to
have more money usually said something to the effect of "to
have more free time." This seems to be the real goal most
MLM distributors are after—not money!

The discrepancy between men and women when it came
to the goal of more money versus more time may not be as
vast as it first appears. Men seemed to answer more from the
gut, with the first thing that popped in their heads. Women

seemed to see money more as a means to an end. They tended to answer more from the heart, with what they wanted to achieve with the money they earned. When men were pressed to think more about their desire for more money, the freedom angle really attracted them as well. I suspect it might actually be at about the same percentage as women.

**Years in MLM: 2.9** Admittedly, I may be responsible for some unintentional data torturing here. Well, more like data irritating actually. Those who would respond to a written survey, which is where most of the data for this question came from, are likely to be a more serious, thus more committed, group overall. I suspect this number might actually be slightly lower. Also, note that this is an average, not a mean. In other words, a few had been in for 10 or 20 years, whereas most had been in for less than 3.

**MLM participation by state (percentage of people within each state who are MLM distributors):**

| Top Ten | | Bottom Ten | |
|---|---|---|---|
| Nevada | 4.22% | Iowa | 0.52% |
| Hawaii | 4.12 | South Dakota | 1.52 |
| Oregon | 4.07 | West Virginia | 1.68 |
| Arizona | 3.95 | Maine | 1.71 |
| Florida | 3.92 | Illinois | 1.81 |
| Washington | 3.81 | North Dakota | 1.89 |
| Utah | 3.51 | Wisconsin | 2.02 |
| Colorado | 3.29 | Kansas | 2.06 |
| Montana | 3.21 | Rhode Island | 2.06 |
| California | 3.17 | South Carolina | 2.12 |

I did more than just define what states had the most MLM distributors. Obviously, the larger states such as California and Texas would come out on top. Instead, I determined what percentage of all MLM distributors were in each state (based on a survey of 17,292 distributors), then figured the total number of distributors in that state, and finally, what percentage of that state's population were MLM distributors. This gives us a better idea of which states are hot and cold MLM states. The obvious conclusion: Go west!

By the way, Texas came in 19th with 2.69%, and New York was 20th with 2.67%. The biggest gainer over the last 4 years is Georgia (from 2.01% to 3.03%). The biggest loser is Arkansas (from 3.03% to 2.21%). In both cases—I have not the slightest clue as to why.

**Average total distributors recruited in MLM career: 2.1**
Here is one of the biggest statistical fallacies in this industry. I've heard other figures ranging from 2.6 to as high as 3. Unfortunately, we fall victim to the same bias as all others who have tried to determine this number. First, we are only surveying current, active distributors. As I mentioned earlier, if everyone who ever participated in MLM over the last 50 years recruited just two, we would have reached worldwide saturation. Also, considering the number of people who participate in two or more programs at once (or who've been in dozens over the years), many of those 2.1 are undoubtedly the same people getting counted more than once. Furthermore, determining an "average" creates the illusion that most or all distributors are recruiting about 2 or 3 peo-

ple. In fact, more than half of all MLM distributors never recruit a soul and drop out within weeks. Many recruit just 1. Very few recruit exactly two people. What causes this average to reach higher than the 2.0 level are those very few who recruit 4, 5, 10, 20 or perhaps more than 100 people. Here's a demonstration of what I mean: Let's say you poll 10 distributors at random and 9 say they've recruited no one. The tenth has recruited 20 people. Therefore, these 10 people have recruited an average of 2 people each, even though no one actually recruited 2 people.

This is why any program that hypes this "if you get two, who only get two" routine, whether it be a two-wide matrix or an Australian (two-up), is using faulty logic. The chances are, the two you get won't get anybody. Also, you won't get any spillover unless you happen to fall under one of those very few who recruit more than two. And the few you do get from spillover, if any, will likely recruit—that's right—no one! Yes, the "average" may be two for all those surveyed, but the most common numbers actually recruited are one—and none.

Actually, it is technically impossible for the recruitment "average" of all distributors to be greater than one. Let's say you are the very first MLM distributor. You recruit two people. There are now three distributors and two recruits. That's an average of 0.67. Now the two you recruit also recruit two. So now seven MLM distributors have recruited a total of six people, but the "average" is only 0.86 people each. Even if every new recruit were to continue to recruit two others, this average would get closer and closer to, but would never reach, 1.0.

**Average number of MLM programs pursued in career: 3.3** You might be surprised at this low number. I certainly was. I found that many distributors were still with their first or second company, however, and only a few had been with several. Those few just seemed to stand out more because they tended to be either well-known veterans of MLM or junkies who had been in dozens of programs. Actually, we found that most new distributors just didn't hang around long enough to involve themselves with more than one or two companies.

On a scale of 1 to 5 (5 being the highest, 3 meaning indifferent, 1 meaning you hate it), various types of product lines were rated like this:

| | | | |
|---|---|---|---|
| Health care | 4.14 | Collectables | 2.77* |
| Skin care | 3.66 | Power/Utilities | 2.70 |
| Cookies/foods | 3.59 | Publications | 2.64 |
| Weight loss | 3.57 | Water/air purifiers | 2.59 |
| Hair care | 3.22 | Automotive | 2.55* |
| Cosmetics | 3.05 | MLM portfolios | 2.48 |
| Benefits packages | 2.99 | Gold/jewelry | 2.46 |
| Pet care | 2.89 | Tax/record keeping | 2.41 |
| Educational | 2.81 | Lead generation | 2.33 |
| Dental/medical | 2.80 | Toys/games | 1.87 |
| Travel | 2.80* | Downline builders | 1.96 |
| Telecommunications | 2.79 | Chain letters | 1.00 |

* Recent additions to survey—figures based on less than 100 responses.

Notice that chain letters never received even one rating of higher than a 1. I'm impressed, but a little skeptical too.

Does this mean no one would ever participate in one, or they have and failed miserably with it?

The only product category that made any significant gain over the last 4 years was telecommunications, but that was likely due to my including Internet access in this category. Gold/jewelry was by far the biggest loser, dropping from 3.21 to 2.46. I'm guessing it had something to do with the fact that my newsletter, in which this survey usually appeared, was very popular with Jewelway distributors (which was attacked by the FTC in 1997 and filed bankruptcy in 1998).

Of course, the real question here is, do distributors claim to prefer health care lines because that's what the company they're involved in sells, or are they involved with these companies because they sell the products they prefer?

What seems to be obvious is that Discovery Toys distributors need to participate in more MLM surveys.

**Number of MLM programs pursued at the same time:**

> One: 55%
> Two: 19%
> Three: 13%
> Four: 5%
> Five or more: 8%

**Record for most opportunities pursued in career: 36**
And this guy is still looking, by the way.

**Record for most opportunities pursued at the same time: 18**   And she's quite proud of it!

Percent of total MLM companies that offer each type of compensation plan (see compensation plan terms in the Appendix for a brief description of each type of plan):

| | |
|---|---|
| Breakaway | 52% |
| Unilevel | 22% |
| Binary | 14% |
| Matrix | 8% |
| Hybrid | 3% |
| Australian (Two-Up) | 1% |

Despite the doomsday predictions of some breakaway bashers, the ol' stair-step still outnumbers every other form of plan combined. However, the percent has dropped 7% from 1990 to 1995 and another 9% from 1996 to 1999. This doesn't mean existing breakaway plans are failing (in fact, most are quite stable). This drop in market share is due more to the massive influx of new start-up companies of which very few are adopting breakaway plans. Matrix plans have also dropped, likely a result of the increase in popularity of the binary plan. Besides the binary, only the unilevel seems to be gaining a slow but steady increase in popularity. Fortunately, Australian plans have never exceeded 1% since I've been keeping track.

**Number of total MLM distributors (United States only):** **7,204,470**   A far cry from the 10 to 15 million we keep hearing about. I computed this figure by adding all the distributor totals for each of the 475 companies in my database (about half are estimates, but they're close estimates). These are the 475 most prominent companies and do not include any that are less than 6 months old. I then assumed that there were 725 more companies with an average of 1,000 distributors each. Considering that the bottom 600 of the 1,200 companies that exist in the United States change over about every 6 months (my estimate), assuming that they all have 1,000 reps is, in fact, absurdly optimistic. I have also added quasi-MLM operations such as Avon and Tupperware to the mix. I did everything I could, within

**The top 1% of all MLM companies (by size) comprise about two thirds of all the distributors!**

reason, to justify the "15 million distributor" claim. I didn't torture the data, I made love to it! And I couldn't even come close to 10 to 15 million.

What is even more revealing is that the top 1% of all MLM companies (by size) comprise about two-thirds of all the distributors! These dozen companies averaged 402,250 distributors each, whereas the other 99% of all MLM companies averaged only 2,001 distributors.

**Actual number of current MLM distributors (United States only): 5,583,464** The most scathing evidence against the "10 to 15 million" claim is that 45% of all network marketers are currently enrolled in more than one MLM program, so we are actually counting about 1.6 million of these folks more than once!

**Total U.S. sales volume: about 4.3 billion** I read an article recently by a well-respected MLM authority who claimed that there were 10 million distributors in the United States moving 20 billion in sales annually. It's amazing that neither he, nor the editors of the very high-profile MLM publication his article appeared in, bothered to do even the most simple mathematical checks on this. For these figures to be true, that would mean the average monthly order of *all* MLM distributors in the country would have to be $168! To assume it's even half that number would be outrageously optimistic. I guessed (and that's all it is) an average of $50, which is still probably on the high side considering at least a third of all distributors currently in a company's "active" list likely aren't ordering anything (some companies take a year to purge inactive reps, and some never do). I also multiplied that $50 by the whole 7.2 million since those who are in more than one company certainly may be ordering product in both. What ever the guesstimate, it's not even close to $20 billion. That's ridiculous.

Not that this is a bad thing. To the contrary. This simply means there's a *lot* more room to grow!

**Top 10 states where MLM companies are based, with number located within each:**

1. California: 92
2. Texas: 71
3. Florida: 50
4. Utah: 26
5. Arizona: 23
6. Nevada: 20
7. Illinois: 17
8. Tennessee: 16
9. Colorado: 14
10. New York: 13

**Oldest MLM companies (as of 1999):**

1. Shaklee: 44 years
2. Neo-Life: 42 years (merged with Diamite Corp.)
3. Amway: 41 years
4. Mary Kay: 37 years
5. NSA: 31 years

---

**Number of MLM companies whose name starts with these letters of the alphabet:**

A: 33
B: 19
C: 32 . . .

Okay, I'm getting ridiculous. Obviously, I've hit the bottom of the barrel as far as MLM-related statistics.

## CONCLUSION

I SUSPECT THE MAJORITY of you reading this book are already involved in network marketing. You are the intended audience. Some of you, however, may have picked up this book as part of your research into MLM—to assist you in deciding whether to join this industry. Although not every page was filled with "happy stuff," I certainly hope I have not dissuaded you from pursuing a good MLM venture. If anything, I hope you have recognized the tremendous potential that network marketing has to improve the lives of millions of Americans—including yours. I hope you now understand and appreciate that we've only scratched the surface of that potential. And most of all, I hope you now understand why.

This book is not about why you should abandon or avoid network marketing. It is about why you should embrace it, love it, support it, respect it, teach it, and help it grow up into the awesome, literally world-changing marvel that it could be. This book is about doing the business, but doing it with awareness and understanding with realistic expectations. It's about doing the business, but doing it with honesty, integrity, and fairness. It's all about doing the business, but doing it right!

Is there a "perfect" MLM opportunity? Probably not. Is there a good, honest program that's trying hard to do right, with a fair compensation plan and good products that are worth the price? Absolutely. Dozens of them.

Other publications, agencies, and organizations can assist you in determining which MLM companies fall into this category. Of course, one good way of determining which opportunities have the least to hide is by judging their acceptance and support of this book! If an MLM distributor handed you this copy, you can pretty much assume his or her opportunity is one of the good ones.

Should you try to find a perfect MLM opportunity? I hope not—unless you're very young. It might take awhile. But if you can find one that's even close, I'll bet you can make it close to perfect for you. Do you hate front-loading? Fine. Don't front-load anybody. Do you hate deceptive opportunity presentations? Don't give them. Do you object to ridiculous medical or income claims? Don't make them. Are you afraid of filling up your garage with unwanted product? Don't buy that much. And you know, being a business of duplication and all, your downline just might follow your example. You see, we are in control of the destiny of network marketing in this country. We can choose to make this business a safer, more dignified, far more rewarding opportunity for average, struggling Americans.

Some of you grizzled veterans of MLM may be thinking, Len, it's just not that simple.

Well, actually, I think it is.

**Subscription Publications**
*MLM Insider/Network Marketing Today*
3529 NE 171st Street
N. Miami, FL 33160
coreya@aol.com

*Fortune Now*
PO Box 57723
Webster, TX 77598
bigalMLM@tntmag.com

*Upline Journal*
106 West South Street
Charlottesville, VA 22902
www.upline.com

*MarketWave Alert Letter*
2406 Canberra Avenue
Henderson, NV 89052
www.marketwaveinc.com
(800) 688-4766

**Other Industry Trade Publications**
*Cutting Edge Opportunities*
1250 Ridge Road
Elizabethtown, PA 17022
www.cuttingedgemedia.com

*Emerald Coast News*
PO Box 190
Niceville, FL 32588
ECNews@aol.com

*Money & Profits*
39 Bowery Street, #919
New York, NY 10002
MNPMag@aol.com

*The Network Trainer*
PO Box 890084
Houston, TX 77289
www.tntmag.com

*Jackpot*
PO Box 6547
Jacksonville, FL 32236
www.jackpotmall.com

*Advantage Networker*
29 John Street, #130
New York, NY 10038
leadmst@aol.com

**Trade Organizations**

Direct Selling Association
1776 K Street, NW, Ste. 600
Washington, DC 20006
www.dsa.org

MLMIA
119 Stanford Court
Irvine, CA 92715

## Productivity Tools

Robert & Joyce Gatchel
(Internet consulting & services)
1241 East 13th Street
Eddystone, PA 19022
electronicmlm@aol.com

PowerLine Systems
(Planner/Organizer)
151 Kalmus Drive, Ste. C-260
Costa Mesa, CA 92626

### Advertising Consultant

Opportunity Connection
17319 Crystal Valley Road
Little Rock, AR 72210

### MLM Start-Up Consultant

Leonard Clements
800-688-4766
www.marketwaveinc.com
(Devil's advocate for hire)

### MLM Attorneys

Grimes & Reese
1270 South Woodruff Ave.
Idaho Falls, ID 83404
kgrimes@nicoh.com

Gerald Nehra
1710 Beach St.
Muskegon, MI 49441
mlmatty@aol.com

## Australian

Unlimited first-level width, infinite depth, linear commissions. This is usually referred to in the United States as a "two-up" plan. The commissions earned by the first two distributors on your first level are passed up to your sponsor. Likewise, the commission from the first two distributors recruited by your third recruit (and on) are passed up to you.

## Binary

First-level width always limited to two, infinite depth, generational commissions. Sometimes referred to as a binary lateral. This plan determines commission payments based on the accumulated sales volume in each of the two legs (group volume under each of the two first-level distributors) usually on a weekly basis. Little consideration is given to actual levels, only the total volume in each leg. The more volume that occurs during the week, the higher the commission payment. Most binary plans pay based on the leg with the least volume, and the excess volume in the strong leg is either carried over to the following week or "flushed" (forfeited). Binary plans generally allow multiple positions by a single distributor.

## Breakaway

Unlimited first-level width, finite depth, generational commissions. When a certain stage of advancement has been reached, based on various qualifications usually involving monthly wholesale personal and group volumes, the distributor and his or her group (downline) "breaks away" from their upline sponsor. This process usually involves eliminating the breakaway group's volume as a source of volume in meeting the upline sponsor's monthly qualifications. Commissions (usually called overrides) can still be earned on this breakaway group once an equivalent or higher stage of advancement has been reached by the upline sponsor.

### Downline
All of those distributors who are within your personal organization. They all branch off from your position in a downward direction.

### Generational Commissions
Commissions are based on the group volume of the distributor on that level. For example, if a breakaway plan paid 5% on level six, this would include the entire group volume of the level six distributor, not just the volume that occurs on the sixth level. This group volume rarely, if ever, includes the volume of other breakaway groups.

### Linear Commissions
Commissions are based on the actual volume that occurs on that specific level.

### Matrix
Limited first-level width (usually 2 to 7 positions), finite depth (usually 5 to 12 levels), linear commissions. Usually all volume that falls within the pay levels counts toward

monthly qualifications. Matrix plans are described by the first-level width limit and the number of levels, for example, a 2 × 12 (no more than two distributors may be placed on your first level, and the plan pays 12 levels deep). All distributors enrolled beyond the first level width limit are placed in deeper levels. This is commonly referred to as "spillover."

## Stair-Step

Any type of plan that has multiple stages or ranks of advancement. For example: Bronze, Gold, and Diamond, or Member, Leader, and Director, and so on. Although any of these plan types can be designated a stair-step, this term rarely precedes any type of plan other than breakaway. All breakaways are "stair-step" breakaways.

## Unilevel

Unlimited first-level width, finite depth (usually five to nine levels), linear commissions. Generally the simplest form of plan. No breakaway occurs, and an unlimited number of distributors can be placed on any level. The term was originally used to describe any type of plan that had only one (uni-) stage (level) of advancement (compared with a stair-step of ranks that could be achieved). Today it is commonly used to describe any nonmatrix, nonbreakaway type of plan regardless of the number of ranks or stages of advancement.

## Upline

The direct line of distributors who are above you in the hierarchy.

Here are some (but not all) of my favorite MLM books.

*Being the Best You Can Be in MLM*, by John Kalench. MIM Publications, San Diego, CA, 1990.

*Big Al Tells All*, by Tom Schreiter. KAAS Publishing, Houston, TX, 1985.

*Financially Free*, by Dennis Windsor. Windward Press, Dallas, TX, 1990.

*Fire Up!* by Jan Ruhe. MLM Publishing, Charlottesville, VA, 1997.

*How to Create a Recruiting Explosion*, by Tom Schreiter. KAAS Publishing, Houston, TX, 1986.

*MLM Magic*, by Venus Andrecht. Ransom Hill Press, Ramona, CA, 1992.

*Network Marketer's Guide to Success*, by J. Babener and D. Stewart. Legaline Publications, Portland, OR, 1990.

*Power Calling*, by Joan Guiducci. Tonino, Mill Valley, CA, 1992.

*Romancing Your Future*, by Philip Stills. Philip Stills Business Books, Santa Rosa, CA, 1994.

*Street Smart Networking*, by Robert Butwin. MLM Publishing, Charlottesville, VA, 1994.

*The Greatest Networker in the World*, by John Milton Fogg. MLM Publishing, Charlottesville, VA, 1992.

*Turbo MLM*, by Tom Schreiter. KAAS Publishing, Houston, TX, 1988.

*Wave 3: The New Era in Network Marketing*, by Richard Poe. Prima Publishing, Roseville, CA, 1993.

*Who Stole the American Dream?* by Burke Hedges. INTI Publications, Tampa, FL, 1993.

*Winning the Greatest Game of All*, by Randy Ward. Cimarron Management Corporation, Jennings, OK, 1990.

# INDEX

L EONARD CLEMENTS WAS born and raised in San Anselmo, CA, just north of San Francisco. He attended Sir Francis Drake High School, where he graduated with honors while finishing in the top 10% in the nation in mathematics. After attending one year of college, he decided to "take a semester off." Six years later he returned to earn his degree in Business Data Processing.

Len's MLM career began in 1979 with a health and nutrition company that, six months later (the same week that he gave notice at his job), went out of business. Len did get his job back, but that swift feeling of success had lit the entrepreneurial fire within him (or, as his original partners in *MarketWave* told him, made him "psychologically unemployable").

After a short stint with two other failed MLM companies, he decided to go the conventional route and opened a computer training and time rental facility in downtown San Francisco. After six profitable years of business (despite numerous thefts, car break-ins, a drug raid on an adjoining business, a suicide outside his front door, two drive-by shootings, and a major earthquake), Len had had enough of "the city."

Len spent a full year doing his homework before reentering the MLM arena and soon discovered that there was a ready and willing market for that same knowledge. He held his first "Facts & Myths of MLM" seminar in his computer classroom in September 1990. Those seminars were a success and soon became a twice monthly event, each time selling out the room. By popular demand of those seminar attendees, the newsletter *MarketWave* was born in January 1991 (then called *Opportunity Knocks*, with a lens of a magnifying glass making the *O* for *Opportunity*).

A prestigious business research and consulting firm in the area was investigating the idea of adding network marketing to its list of "low-risk" business opportunities for its clients. A representative of this firm attended one of Len's seminars in early February of the same year. As a result, Len was hired as its senior market analyst, and within weeks a separate, entirely MLM-focused division was created and called MarketWave. Later that year Len sold his computer business and purchased MarketWave outright.

MarketWave has remained an unaffiliated, objective information clearinghouse for the network marketing industry ever since. Len routinely puts in 50- to 60-hour work weeks writing his "Inside Network Marketing" column, providing telephone consulting, and conducting his "Facts & Myths of MLM" seminars throughout the United States, Canada, and Mexico. He currently holds a position as a distributor for a prominent MLM company (which has never been named in the pages of *MarketWave*, or in this book) and fully intends to continue his duties as one of the "watchdogs" of network marketing. For more information about MarketWave, call 800-688-4766.

Len currently resides in Henderson, Nevada. He plans to return to the Bay Area someday—but not to San Francisco.

# To Order Books

Please send me the following items:

| Quantity | Title | Unit Price | Total |
|---|---|---|---|
| _____ | **Heart to Heart** | $ _____ | $ _____ |
| _____ | **Street Smart Network Marketing** | $ _____ | $ _____ |
| _____ | _____ | $ _____ | $ _____ |
| _____ | _____ | $ _____ | $ _____ |
| _____ | _____ | $ _____ | $ _____ |

| | |
|---|---|
| Subtotal | $ _____ |
| 7.25% Sales Tax (CA only) | $ _____ |
| 7% Sales Tax (PA only) | $ _____ |
| 5% Sales Tax (IN only) | $ _____ |
| 7% G.S.T. Tax (Canada only) | $ _____ |
| Priority Shipping | $ _____ |
| Total Order | $ _____ |

## FREE
### Ground Freight
### in U.S. and Canada

Foreign and all Priority Request orders:
Call Customer Service
for price quote at 916-787-7000

**By Telephone:** With American Express, MC, or Visa,
call 800-632-8676, Monday–Friday, 8:30–4:30.
**www.primapublishing.com**
**By E-mail:** sales@primapub.com
**By Mail:** Just fill out the information below
and send with your remittance to:

**Prima Publishing ▪ P.O. Box 1260BK ▪ Rocklin, CA 95677**

Name _____

Address _____

City _____ State _____ ZIP _____

American Express/MC/Visa# _____ Exp. _____

Check/money order enclosed for $ _____ Payable to Prima Publishing

Daytime telephone _____

Signature _____